The
DONNIE DARKO
Book

Richard Kelly (photo: Jaron Presant)

The
DONNIE DARKO
Book

RICHARD KELLY

faber and faber

First published in 2003
by Faber and Faber Limited
3 Queen Square London WC1N 3AU
Published in the United States by Faber and Faber Inc.
an affiliate of Farrar, Straus and Giroux LLC, New York

Typeset by Country Setting, Kingsdown, Kent CT14 8ES
Printed in England by Mackays of Chatham plc, Chatham, Kent

Photos from film courtesy of Metrodome Distribution Ltd.

Images from 'They Made Me Do It' Exhibition
courtesy of theymademedoit.com

Sketches courtesy of Richard Kelly

The Philosophy of Time Travel created by Hi-Res!
as part of donniedarko.com (http://www.donniedarko.com)
Creative Directors: Florian Schmitt/Alexandra Jugovic

Photos from film and from behind the scenes
taken by Dale Robinette

This book would not have been possible without
the generous assistance of Tom Grievson

A CIP record for this book
is available from the British Library

ISBN 0-571-22124-6

6 8 10 9 7 5

Contents

Richard Kelly in the movie theatre
with Jake Gyllenhaal, Jena Malone, and Frank.

Foreword

by Jake Gyllenhaal

What is *Donnie Darko* about? I have no idea, at least not a conscious one. But somehow I've always understood it. The most amazing thing about making this movie, for me, was the fact that no one – including the man from whose mind it emerged – ever had a simple answer to this question. And that, ironically, is the very thing the film is actually about. There is no single answer to any question. Every person's explanation differs according to how they were brought up, where they were brought up, who brought them up. This seems like a very simple answer to a perplexingly complex movie, but when you think about it, it gets to the very crux of what we all seem to take for granted: our own minds, how they differ, and that we are all entitled to our own interpretation.

The struggle begins when, at a certain age, a kid starts to experience the effects of his childhood and the possibility that his upbringing was flawed. It's hard to accept the idea that there is no ideal. Nothing is perfect. The hardest part, though, is when he or she begins the search for his or her own idea of what is right. It's scary to search. You never know what resistance you might meet.

America is a culture that prides itself on supporting this kind of inquiry but, in fact, it often inhibits self-expression. Too often we are encouraged to be passive, not to challenge our leadership, not to inquire too far. And popular culture often reflects this passive relationship. Kids know when it's Britney Spears's birthday, but they probably couldn't tell you the name of America's Vice-President. Not to diss Britney Spears: I think she's hot. I bought her last record. And not to diss Dick Cheney either: he's provided a lot more drama than some of our leading screen-writers. But who's to blame?

None of this is our fault. We are a product of our culture. But we can't be afraid to speak our minds.

And it is this that makes *Donnie Darko* so cool. Richard Kelly used the backdrop of the 80s, a mainstream style of filmmaking (his hero is Spielberg – who rocks, by the way) against itself, to be subversive. To give us something different from what we're used to. In the words of Donnie himself, 'to change things'.

Call it cult. Call it genius. Call it what you will, but the fact that Richard has chosen not to spoon-feed his audience a simple conclusion to the film requires his audience to participate in the process of figuring it out with him.

There aren't a whole lot of people doing this.

When we were working, I would beg and plead with Richard to find one through-line and an understandable conclusion. He never would. Some could argue this was detrimental to the film. And it might be to any other film. And there are those who would say that it was to this one. But I wish those people could spend a day with me sometime. So they could sit at a meal, or walk down the street when a total stranger walks up and starts a philosophical discussion about what exactly *Donnie Darko* is about. It makes my day every time. Because every time, I answer, 'I have no idea, what does it mean to you?'

New York City, 4 May 2003

Asking Cosmic Questions

Richard Kelly interviewed by Kevin Conroy Scott

KEVIN CONROY SCOTT *You have described your upbringing in Richmond, Virginia, as being 'very normal'. What does 'normal' mean to you?*

RICHARD KELLY It was normal in the sense that I came from a very functional family; my parents are still together, they're not divorced. Divorce is the first crisis most kids encounter, and luckily I never had to go through that. We had enough money to get by, we lived in a nice neighbourhood, we never feared for our lives. I think a lot of art comes out of anguish or pain, so a privileged upbringing can stifle artistic impulses, and indeed there was very little for me to rebel against where I grew up. When there isn't much to feel anguished about, you have to search in other places for your art. I don't know, I guess I found my art among the mundane.

You have often been very complimentary of your parents, even going as far as giving them much of the credit for your success to this date. Why are they so important?

They saw something in me and they really encouraged me. They liked my drawings and put them up on the refrigerator. They saw that I might have the ability to draw and they put me in an art class when I was five years old. I think that is an unusual thing, particularly when you grow up in a conservative town like Richmond. My parents weren't artists but they were really aggressive about pushing me into that world. Ultimately, I think that was what gave me the confidence and motivation to be a filmmaker. Throughout my entire life they told me to use my art because they thought I had a talent there. They encouraged me to make a career out of my artistic abilities.

What kind of artistic activities did they encourage you to get involved with?

My mother really pushed me into writing. She always told me that I had an ability to write and was very effective in her ability to make me a better writer. She was a teacher and a very good editor and critic of papers I would write. I think I got my writing sensibility from my mother and my mathematical sensibility from my father.

Your father helped design the first camera to photograph Mars. Can you tell me something about his profession and his interests?

For a number of years, my dad worked for NASA down in Norfolk, Virginia. We were the first family on the block to get a computer; we had the Apple II, then the Apple II Plus; it was upgraded every year. There was always an appreciation of technology in our house. My dad was always rebuilding something or fixing my mom's car; he was always the handy craftsman or the engineer. It definitely gave me the confidence, or the ability, to be a kind of technician or craftsman. I think that's pretty much what a filmmaker is, and I definitely got that from my father. Seeing the work he did at NASA, I can't even understand some of the things he built. It's unheralded and forgotten work that a lot of those guys did back then in the Viking lander days in 1976. They photographed Mars for the first time. They didn't know what they were going to see transmitted back in the photographs. There was apprehension about little green men; ultimately they found out it was just a red desert with a bunch of rocks.

What kind of high school did you attend?

I went to a public school called Midlothian High School. It was a really good school. I am thankful that I did not have the privilege of a private education. I think that private school can sometimes create an elitist world view. I'm glad that I am not a by-product of that. In a way, public school prepared me for the evil in the world. Nothing prepares you for the evil in the world like high school.

Your mother was a teacher of emotionally disturbed students. Can you tell me something about her job?

Mostly it was getting her students to do their homework. When I was in junior high she was the in-school suspension teacher, which means that when kids were suspended but still had to come to school, they had to go and sit with my mom, all day. So that means she was not a psychotherapist for kids who were trying to kill themselves or stab each other. She was the caretaker for the bad seeds.

How was her reputation with the bad seeds?

She was very well liked. For someone in that position it was easy to get a negative reputation, but my mom is an extremely kind person.

The 'Mad World' drawing featured in the film and in the music video
for the song, drawn by Richard Kelly in high school.

Actually, some of my closest friends ended up in suspension a lot. It was a little awkward, her knowing that I was hanging out with the 'bad seeds'. I mean it was just junior high; junior high is altogether stupid. But still, you could start to see the roots of dysfunction in all of us.

You were a big Stephen King fan as a teenager. Can you explain your attraction to his work?

I was just floored by his imagination. I think one of the first novels I ever read was *Carrie*. Everything that I read, other than Stephen King, I found to be far less imaginative. A lot of people are critical of King because he is considered a popular fiction writer. The critical community seems to be dismissive of popular fiction, but I challenge anyone to come up with a science-fiction, fantasy or horror writer with a larger imagination than Stephen King.

What do you think are some of the best feature-film adaptations of his novels?

Clearly *The Shawshank Redemption*; Rob Reiner did a spectacular job with William Goldman's adaptation of *Misery*, and with *Stand By Me* . . . Rob Reiner has a great way of keying into the humanity of King's work. De Palma's *Carrie*. Cronenberg's *The Dead Zone*. I think *Dolores Claiborne* was a great adaptation. I would love to produce a re-make of *It* or *The Tommyknockers* as an HBO mini-series. Those books were not serviced well by ABC. I hope one day to be able to convince King to let me adapt *The Long Walk*. I think that is one of his greatest accomplishments as a writer, although I hear he has tried to discontinue its publication. Some people have been critical of Kubrick's interpretation of *The Shining*, but I think it is one of the greatest horror films ever made.

Why did you like The Shining *so much?*

I'm a Kubrick fanatic. No one else has ever done a haunted house, let alone a hotel, as well as he did. He created a physical environment that truly is a character in the film. Every time I watch it, it gets more interesting. I think a lot of people fail to see the humanity in that film, the black comedy in that film. Ultimately I think Kubrick made a series of black comedies. I think that people were so disturbed or taken with the technical side of what he was doing they failed to see

'Wilted Flower': another of Kelly's high-school drawings which featured in the film.

the humanity and the comedy. If you look at something like *Barry Lyndon*, it is an absolutely breathtaking technical achievement with the zoom lenses and candle-lit interiors courtesy of NASA, but it is also an accomplished piece of social criticism.

About social climbing?

Yes, about social climbing. Just the portrait of a jackass; a jackass who destroys everything and everyone around him.

You were also interested in the time-travel theorist Stephen Hawking. He's not as popular a choice with the teenage set as the other Stephen.

Right. In eighth grade I was asked to do a book report in science class and I picked *A Brief History of Time* because I thought it had a cool title. I couldn't understand a word of it. I only understood a few sentences, but I was so inspired by someone who clearly understood the world on a completely different level – and could express it in words. Even though I could not comprehend it, it inspired me to try and comprehend it and, as a result, that book has been in the back of my mind ever since. I think you are challenged by things that are slightly beyond your grasp.

Were you reading literary fiction in high school? Graham Greene surfaces in Donnie Darko.

Most of my true literary education came in high school. Kafka, Dostoevsky, Faulkner, Camus, Graham Greene.

Were you a voracious reader in high school?

I was in an accelerated English class and we had to read the writers I just mentioned. Thank God. I would never have read any of those books had I not been required to because I was a lazy student. I did the bare minimum to get by. I actually started to enjoy reading something other than Stephen King. That really taught me how to tell a story: King and then all those other writers I just mentioned.

So King showed you how to write a thumping narrative?

In a way, yes. King taught me suspense and how to create a fantasy world. Also, how to terrify an audience, how to move them, how to do all the great things that King can do. I think these writers like Dostoevsky, Camus and Greene taught me history and social criticism and also structure, more than anything. The math of storytelling came from those great writers. Joseph Campbell's mythology work is spot-on. Its influence is undeniable in Hollywood films, but it should be embraced in the sense that you learn the formula, then you learn how to corrupt that formula.

What about comic books? I know you mentioned something in the DVD commentary about Donnie Darko's *relationship to comic books.*

I was never a gigantic comic-book guy; I had a passing interest in comic books. But when I wrote the title, *Darko*, it sounded like a comic book. It was also meant to delve into the archetypes of suburbia. When you are aware that you are delving into archetypes that have become clichés – especially teen films and coming-of-age stories – you push into the comic-book realm. It made sense for the way I was trying to tell a story about teenagers and suburbia – it was meant to have a sardonic element. I don't know how well I communicated that, but I think that was the intention.

When you first saw the music video for Aerosmith's 'Janie's Got a Gun' you rang up MTV's office and asked who directed it. How old were you then and why did you do that?

That was 1989 and I was fourteen years old. I saw the video and I thought, 'That person has a vision. That's a movie, I want to see that movie.' That was in the stage of my teens when all I was doing was watching MTV. I had never seen a video that told a story. It was better crafted than most movies I had seen and I was taken aback by it and I wanted to know who created it. At that point they did not have the director's names on music videos so I called up the MTV offices and

Richard Kelly's family home in Midlothian, Virginia.

got ten different recordings and finally got someone who told me it was David Fincher and then they hung up on me. And then I found out that he was doing the third *Alien* film, which freaked me out because the first two *Alien* films were my favourite films of all time. I thought, 'Well, I'm glad someone else saw something there.' And despite the troubles he endured, I think *Alien³* is a vastly underrated film. I hear that Fox is going to release his original cut on DVD.

When did being a director become a tangible idea for you to pursue as a career? Was it at that point?

That inspired me – in the sense that I thought I would love to be that good a filmmaker, to take my art to that level. In Fincher's work I saw an unparalleled level of craftsmanship that spoke to me and my hope and dream of expressing myself artistically. When I see something that is really good it makes me want to try and do something really good too. I don't know why it was that video, but it was. It inspired me to make movies.

You have said that the holy trinity that crystallised your love for movies was, 'E.T., Back to the Future, Aliens. Spielberg, Zemeckis, Cameron: they were the ones who made me want to sneak out of the house and into R-rated films.' Looking back on that period of your life, can you try to remember why you found those films so captivating?

When you grow up in Richmond and there is no such thing as DVD and no one you know owns a laserdisc player, all you have are the films that are available at your local Blockbuster, and even then Blockbuster was in its infancy. So I certainly wasn't aware of *The Bicycle Thief* or *Kurosawa's Dreams*. I didn't have access to Truffaut, so I couldn't go rent *Day for Night*; it wasn't available at Odyssey Video on Midlothian Turnpike. All I had access to were the big block-buster films. There was nothing better, in my eyes, than what Cameron, Spielberg and Zemeckis were doing.

The East Coast is home to some fine universities. Why did you decide to go so far away from home for university?

I thought it was my chance to get away from home and go somewhere far away. I thought, 'Why not go to Los Angeles?' It sounded like an adventure and I wanted to have an adventure. In the back of my mind

I thought maybe I'd try and get into the movie business one day. If I didn't, I thought I would always have that regret, so I just went there.

What were some of your first impressions of the place?

I literally showed up alone with two suitcases. I never visited before that. I got to see the 'hood right away. The University of Southern California is like an oasis of spoiled children right in the middle of the ghetto. That, to me, was really interesting – the disparity of a college girl in a BMW parking in front of a crack house. You saw that every day. There is no way to relive that moment when you first walk into a new city and it is really fresh; your take on the geography, your take on the environment is completely new – there is something very exciting in that.

What was your original major at USC?

It was Fine Arts; I got an art scholarship, which I held on to. I dropped the art major after two days, became undeclared, started taking film classes, applied to film school, then got in.

Was film school part of your undergraduate work?

Yes, I didn't go to grad school.

Richard Kelly with parents Lane and Ennis at his graduation from USC Film School, May 1997.

When did you starting making short films?

My true coursework began my junior year of college. The curriculum required us to make five Super-8 shorts. The first film was called *The Vomiteer* starring my friend Marty Mischel. It was about a guy who can't stop vomiting: it destroys his life, he can't hold down a job, can't keep a girlfriend after he barfs on her boobs; he eventually tries to kill himself by swallowing his vomit, but then he decides to live. One of my professors had to get up and leave the room because the film actually made her vomit. So it's very clear from the beginning what my aspirations were. That professor did gave me an A– though.

Do you know why you chose that subject?

I think it was probably a reaction to the pretension I saw within film school and my desire to learn the craft, the technique, but not be pretentious. I think self-importance is a problem for a lot of film students: to solve the world's problems or the desire to make people weep. Comedy is so undervalued and looked down upon, but it is so needed. If you can tell a simple comedic story you can then do anything. If you look at some of Spike Jonze's shorts, they're simple and funny and now he can do anything. The hardest thing to do is to get a good laugh out of someone.

Do you remember anything you learned from making those student films?

More than anything I learned to try and tell a story in an unconventional way, because so much of what I saw at USC appeared conventional to me. I try to make it my mandate to be original and unconventional in the process of delivering a story to someone. Another thing I learned was that when you are conceiving a film the first person you have to please is yourself. If you are trying to please other people, you are never going to have a voice of your own. It's never going to be a film that comes from an honest place. Since the beginning I've always tried to create things that I wanted to see but I haven't seen before.

You've said that when you came out of film school you were broke, so you started writing because you needed the money. However, Donnie Darko *does not feel like a screenplay that was written to make money.*

I didn't write *Donnie Darko* to make money. I basically wrote what I thought was going to be my first film. Luckily, I got an agent off of it.

I didn't start writing for purely mercenary reasons until after I got an agent and I needed to pay the bills while I was struggling to get my movie made. I adapted a novel for a company and then I sold a pilot to the Fox network and did some of that kind of stuff. It was a good experience in the art of negotiation and the art of confrontation with studio executives and people like that.

Did you learn about screenwriting at USC?

I took one screenwriting class, but I really knew nothing about screenwriting when I started writing *Darko*. At that point I'd probably read three scripts in my life. I'm glad I didn't take a lot of screenwriting courses. I wouldn't have even bothered writing *Donnie Darko* if I'd had a bunch of screenwriting rhetoric pushed on me because I would have thought, 'I'm not allowed to do this, I'm not allowed to do that.' Screenwriting courses can be beneficial to some people; I just know it wouldn't have been beneficial to me. My high-school English class informed my screenwriting ability more than anything I learned at film school.

Terry Gilliam and Peter Weir are both heroes of yours. You have said, 'They both look at the metaphysics of life, making films that ask cosmic questions.' What did you mean by that?

To me both of those guys, in completely different ways, are delving into a metaphysical plane. Look at something like *Picnic at Hanging Rock*. Where did those girls go? Look at *Fearless*. Weir's trying to grasp a piece of the unknown through human experience. Look at *Brazil*, look at *Twelve Monkeys*, look at *The Fisher King*. In a sense Gilliam is, ironically, making these Don Quixote fables. In a way he has already made his Don Quixote film. This searching and trying to grasp for something that is unobtainable – these guys are doing it in completely different ways but I think there is a link there and that is my inspiration.

You met your producer Sean McKittrick in college. Can you tell me something about how you met and how your working relationship evolved?

I was friends with an actress named Sasha Alexander who I asked to be in my grad film; I also asked her to produce it. She accepted the acting invitation, but told me she did not have time to produce it. She was working on the Sony lot and Sean was an intern there, so she recommended him and it turned out we had a bunch of mutual friends. We had the same sensibility, we liked the same movies. I am only successful working with people I would hang out with in a social situation and it worked out that Sean and I got along very well. He is a very detail-orientated, organised, responsible person whereas I am messy, irresponsible and a scatterbrain. It's just nice to have a producing partner who can pick up the slack and do things that you are not able to do yourself.

What was the experience like, directing your grad film?

I had written this ridiculous script about a mad scientist and a teleportation chamber. It was called *Visceral Matter*. The intention was to do a *Mystery Science Theatre* kind of thing – only with really good cinematography, set design, visual effects, computer animation, digital matte paintings . . . the whole works. Sean read it and said: 'This is stupid. I love it. Let's go make it.' It was essentially us testing ourselves to see if we could pull together a really elaborate, professional-looking 35-millimetre project with visual effects for very little money.

The summer of 1997 we went out to the desert with a bunch of struggling actors – some of whom we pulled off of Venice Beach when we saw their headshots hanging in a bar. We were desperate to find anyone who could be our renegade team of mad scientists. So we go out to Barstow to shoot the desert footage . . . because the teleportation chamber is buried beneath this gigantic compound and a corporation called Norcom wanted to find it, right? Poor Sasha Alexander – who had agreed to play Karen Chambers, the sexy babe scientist with a secret agenda – got lost on the way to the set because we didn't print up directions properly. She was stranded in the middle of the desert for about an hour. Then – when she was in the Winnebago changing into costume – one of the actors that we pulled off Venice Beach to play one of the Norcom goons kept pulling down his pants and exposing himself to her. It was really creepy. Thankfully, she still speaks to me. I am happy that she has done well for herself.

The next day we shot on Edwards Airforce Base without permits. Military jets were flying overhead and they saw us out in the desert and called the military police. They threatened to arrest us and take our footage. My cameraman Jaron Presant had to hide the footage from them. Somehow we talked ourselves out of it.

So then we head back to LA to shoot in the teleportation chamber – which my production designer Leslie Keel and I had spent the entire summer building in my garage in Hermosa Beach. We then assembled the large pieces on a stage in North Hollywood. It was insane. I slept in this teleportation chamber set for about four days . . . maybe two hours of sleep each night.

So we wrap production and I have all of this footage, a lot of it green screen footage – and I have no money! – no way to finish the film. Sean goes off and gets a job in development at New Line Cinema. I go off and get a job as a client assistant at a post-production house called 525. A 'client assistant' is really a waiter, runner and a janitor for all of the staff and the music video directors, ad execs and rock stars who come through.

I desperately needed to find an editor. They let the client assistants 'train' at night on the Avids once you've worked there for three months. That was my plan – find one of the CAs who knew the Avid to edit the film for me . . . for no money. Because I had no money left. I conned a few of the CAs into looking at the footage – and none of the dialogue was in synch. Hours and hours of work. It was going to be an enormous technical undertaking. Two or three people came and went within the span of two weeks. I figured . . . this film is never going to be completed. This is a disaster.

So then I get a call from Sam Bauer, one of the CAs who worked the night shift. He said, 'I hear you have this trippy science-fiction film and you need an editor. I'm training on the Avid and I'm interested in the job.' I warned him that there was no money, that it was going to take months to finish. He didn't care. He wanted to do it. It was like that scene in *Private Parts* when Howard Stern is still struggling and he drops all of his records on the floor and he starts freaking out and Fred very calmly helps him pick them up and reorganize them.

So during the day Sam and I are fetching food and making cappuccinos, cheese-cracker plates for Puff Daddy, Jennifer Lopez, Weird Al Jankovich, Madonna, Mark Romanek, Jonas Akerlund, Missy Elliott. All of these celebrities. I remember Puff Daddy's bodyguards were inspecting his food. We didn't understand why they thought we would want to poison him or Jennifer Lopez. It was pretty bizarre. I made a cheese-cracker plate for Mark Romanek and now I am friends with him and we have the same agent.

Sam Bauer (left) and Richard Kelly at the Los Angeles première
of *Donnie Darko.*

For months Sam and I burned the midnight oil editing this ridiculous, intentionally awful film that looked gorgeous. Sean was slaving away at New Line for an executive named Lynn Harris . . . learning the business, checking in now and then on our progress. We promised Sam that if I ever got a feature he would edit it. Two years later, Pandora was refusing to let me have him edit *Darko* and Sean and I had to fight like hell to get him the job. Eventually they caved in. Sam Bauer got the job.

You wrote Donnie Darko *during this time period shortly after graduating from film school in 1997. Where did the idea start? I think I remember reading something about a piece of ice falling off a jet engine . . .*

I think that was the seed of the whole idea. It comes back to my high-school English class where we were told that every story was built around a single conceit. If you read *The Metamorphosis,* the conceit is in the first sentence. For me the jet engine was the conceit and then the quest was for me to solve the mystery of the jet engine. Then I just tried to find the most interesting voyage to solve that mystery. That was the process for me. I didn't know how I would get there, but

I knew that engine would come off his mother's plane, in another dimension. I tried to establish some ground rules and then I tried to find the most entertaining way of getting that jet engine to fall from that plane.

Donnie Darko combines some very strong elements: an idealised suburban setting, the 1980s period and a unique protagonist. Can you take me through your discovery process? In which order did the components come into play?

There was the requirement for me of getting his mother on that plane and there was always a messenger figure – a guide, a mentor – who would help his mother get on that plane. Then there was a car accident, and these things were going to build into a cataclysm that would put Donnie into a situation where he has no choice but to realign things by putting this engine back in place. Honestly, it was written so quickly, I can never really explain how I put it all together.

You didn't get stuck at all during that writing process?

Nancy Juvonen and Sean McKittrick on set.

No. I just kept writing. I never stopped to change anything, it just came out. It was really long, 150 pages, but it was very close to what you see in the finished film. It would never be what it is if I had stopped and second-guessed myself because I probably would have gotten scared. Everyone has that post-college meltdown where they are second-guessing every decision they make as they are taking their first uncertain steps towards adulthood. It was written in that moment.

You've done a lot of writing since. When a screenplay is not working the way you want it to, how do you handle the moments of self-doubt during the writing process?

I do one of two things: I go to a bar or I go to the gym. The only way I can deal with that anxiety is to be a normal person and to go out and be social or go exercise. Being by myself only perpetuates that feeling of anxiety. Writing can be a very lonely profession, so when I am not writing I need to be around people.

You said, 'I wanted to communicate the idea that this is a fantasy, a fable, right up front. But it's an intense one – a comic-book archetype of a kid who loses it.' If it is a fantasy, why did you make the depiction of Donnie's life so realistic?

That's the thing with fantasy, why it is so difficult to do. For me, for fantasy to truly work, there has to be an undercurrent of absolute realism. If you are going to have time portals, a bunny rabbit and liquid spears growing out of people's chests, if you are pushing in such a fantastic direction, you have to ground it in a realistic portrayal. Otherwise, these fantastic elements are going to collapse. That became the rule in my head. The way we shot certain things, we tried to have a high degree of naturalism so that the fantastic elements were not off-balance.

Donnie Darko is diagnosed as borderline schizophrenic. Did exposure to your mother's work with the 'bad seeds' have any influence on constructing his character?

I would always overhear my mom talking about it, but she would never talk about it in front of me. I actually remember this guy, when I was thirteen or fourteen years old, who was in my class even though he was eighteen years old. We were in Home Economics class and we could see white powder in his nostrils. He would be sniffing and

Kelly on set – a lonely profession.

coughing and rubbing his nose and was totally coked up and we would stare at him in morbid fascination and ask each other, 'Whoa, what's that like?' Our teacher thought he had a cold. She had no idea he was really coked up. We were really frightened by this guy but at the same time completely fascinated by him and his otherness.

For me, ambiguity is a big reason why your film was so successful. Were you ever tempted to give the audience more information when you were writing so they could connect the dots more easily? For example, my first time viewing the film I was not aware that Donnie had saved his community from an apocalyptic destruction.

When I was writing the script I was so afraid that if I clarified the ending any more than I did, the film would collapse under its own pretension. I was terrified of the whole thing becoming a completely pretentious enterprise. Who knows if I succeeded in avoiding that, but when you are delving into 'Big Ideas' you run the risk of having the whole thing explode in your face. Out of respect for the audience and not wanting to alienate any number of them, I chose to only go so far in answering the questions that the film raises. To come out and say, 'It was all a dream' or, 'It was all about God' – those are codas that always bother me in films. Life isn't all about one thing. I also have to give a lot of credit to Sean McKittrick, Nancy Juvonen and Jake Gyllenhaal. They were very aggressive and vocal in not letting there be one simple answer or one simple solution. I'm so thankful they were supportive in that, because the film would have collapsed and become unwatchable and pretentious had we tagged it with a single solution. But it bothers other people that there is not a single, simple solution. There are certain people in the audience that come to the cinema and want to know exactly what it all meant. Unfortunately for them, this isn't ever going to be one of those movies.

In a similar way, you never show Donnie's superhero powers in action during the first two-thirds of the film. How big a decision was it for you to make a sci-fi movie with a superhero without showing any of his super powers in action?

It would have been cheesy to see Donnie levitating and swinging an axe into a statue. It would have been over the top. We tried to retain the mystery of it with the old adage of 'less is more'. We were just very careful about what we chose to show and what we chose to hide. A lot of times it does come down to budget. I fear what I might do when I get too much money. I'll probably make something awful.

Restriction of budget also worked effectively for the makers of The Blair Witch Project.

Yes, and *Jaws* too. Well, with *Jaws* it was not really restrictions of the budget; the shark wouldn't work. They could barely show the shark, which made it even better.

Where did the idea of the Cunning Visions *infomercials come from?*

That was all recreated from stuff we were exposed to in eighth and ninth grade. We were taught a very similar curriculum to that and I was mocking that. We shot the infomercials at Patrick Swayze's ranch in Calabassas. It was so much fun directing those infomercials. There was our DP, Steven Poster, who has lit a Ridley Scott film, trying to light an infomercial so it looks cheesy but still kind of beautiful in its cheesiness. Trying to do something with that disparity was a thrill for him. I love making infomercials; I want to make the greatest infomercial ever.

The period music you use in the film – The Church, Echo and The Bunnymen, Tears for Fears – was very effective and evocative of that era. At what point during the writing process did music become integral to the narrative?

There was an INXS song written into the script, in the opening, and a Tears for Fears song written in somewhere else. Those two were planned as musical sequences. When a song is used in a film – I'm thinking of *Pulp Fiction* or *GoodFellas* or *Boogie Nights* – you can see the film come to life in a new way. The images and the music work together like a great tango and it is really magical. I figured there were opportunities in this story to put a musical code on the character's experience within this era. Picking those songs was, on our part, not to do with making it campy and mocking of the 1980s. The film was mocking that period, so we did not want the music to mock it as well. We wanted the music to be sincere.

Do you listen to music when you are writing?

Yes, all the time. I listen to tons of music. What I've started to do now is, I make a CD to accompany the script. I put songs in the script and I ask people listen to the CD when they read it.

Does it help establish the tone?

Definitely. You can see the movie; you can hear it while you are reading it. It also helps you communicate your vision if you can do it with music. I use classical music; sometimes I use a temp score from another picture, and sometimes I'll listen to a score from another film on my Walkman when I am writing. That is very effective.

I thought the first dinner-table scene, where the family sits down for pizza and discusses politics, sets the tone for the film. I was wondering where the dialogue came from, particularly the banter about 'fuck-ass' and 'suck a fuck'.

This interview is becoming so academic! Two of my fraternity brothers, Bill Endemann and Justyn Wilson, used to get into these vicious insult wars and it would always devolve into creative combinations of curse words – and 'fuck-ass' was one that stuck with me. I must give credit to them for that. There is something inane about bizarre combinations of cuss words. For a family, what began as a political discussion devolved into a discourse of 'What's a fuck-ass?' It just seemed to cover the spectrum of conversation at a family meal.

I also thought it was very interesting because it says something about the parents. They are more insulted by the political comments about voting for Michael Dukakis than by the word 'fuck-ass' being used in front of their nine-year-old daughter.

That's not the family I grew up in, but to me there is something interesting about a family that is so liberal in their lack of inhibition yet politically very conservative. There is something interesting about that dichotomy because I do think it exists: an environment where a family is completely open with language and sexuality, where the children would have the confidence to completely disagree with their parents about politics. Unknowingly, the parents have created an open-minded, liberal environment in a politically conservative household; they have created their own liberal monsters. It is an unusual disparity, but it was intentional. The traditional way of doing conservative Republican parents is that they don't let their children cuss. A lot of people in Hollywood are very liberal and it is very easy to bash conservative people. I come from a family of conservatives. I come from the land of Republicans. These are people that I love and care about. You have to respect both sides of the political system. You have to respect both parties and even though you may disagree with many of the things a party stands for, you have to try and come to an understanding of why someone thinks that way, otherwise you are never going to come to a solution. I did not want to demonise a character because they are conservative or they are Republican. That would be condescending and as a storyteller it is not my responsibility to push a political ideology on somebody by demonising one side. I wanted to make sure the audience loved those two parents.

Did you have any problems writing the role of the psychiatrist? It's a limited role, emotionally, due to the restrictive nature of the doctor–patient relationship.

The role of Dr Thurman builds to the final scene which, for me, is the most emotional scene in the film. When Donnie is hypnotised you see the terror in her eyes, you see her trying to grapple with what this kid is going through. Their last scene together has the most emotional dialogue in the film. Katharine Ross delivered the dialogue with great restraint, which I have to commend her for. She brought a gravity and a dignity to the role. It's always a brave choice for an actor to underplay something instead of overdoing it. The film was juggling so many balls in the air that any performance that was over the top would have made the film collapse. Any time I sensed that we were running the risk of being too cartoonish, I made sure we pulled back and restrained ourselves. The only thing I regret about the therapist scenes is that there is a sub-plot about her giving Donnie placebos instead of medication. I wished that was still in the film because that would have helped resolve her intentions.

Which would say what about her character?

That she does not think Donnie is crazy. She's been trying to get to the root of his problems through psychology, not medication, to get him to expose things under the assumption that the medication is making him better when really he is making himself better, naturally, without drugs.

You have said in many interviews that you are not Donnie Darko. However, Donnie tells his new girlfriend that he wants to be a writer or a painter, two skills of yours that are on display in this film. So surely the character of Donnie Darko is at least partly autobiographical?

I'll concede that there are many parts of me that are in that character. But I have never been diagnosed as being mentally ill. However, there are a lot of parts of Donnie that are a part of me. That's inevitable. Art is personal. For me, all the artists I admire expose themselves. It's a dangerous thing to expose yourself because you always run the risk of everyone seeing what a big jerk you are. It's a dangerous and frightening thing, but if you are going to do this for a living and be good at it, you have to be willing to expose yourself.

The conversation about the Smurfs lightens the tone of the picture and brings some comic relief at a crucial juncture of the narrative, just before the climactic events of Halloween. Where did the idea for the scene come from?

I think I actually had that conversation with some friends at one point. Growing up, everyone was obsessed with the Smurfs at a certain age. There has been a Smurf backlash. There are a lot of websites that claim that the Smurfs are communists or Satanists. There is a cultural fascination with that cartoon. For whatever reason it became an inane conversation about the teenage obsession with sex, referencing a controversial cartoon that is also a cultural touchstone. There is more going on there than just a flippant Tarantino-wannabe dialogue scene. There is intended to be a social subtext to that scene; I don't know if anyone picked up on that, but that's what I was trying to do.

Can you tell me something about how you approached the scene where Donnie taps his knife on the mirror and looks at Frank across his bathroom mirror?

The idea behind the bathroom scenes was to create an environment that houses Frank. I always wondered as a kid watching a movie: what happens when you try and touch a ghost or an apparition? If you kept seeing one, wouldn't you eventually try and touch it? In my mind it sounded logical for there to be some sort of construct that is housing that apparition. For me that construct was a barrier of water. I tried to address the metaphysics behind the water-barrier idea in the time-travel book. To try and articulate that logic in the movie would have been way too much. It would be a twelve-hour film!

How did you design the digital shots, such as when the spear leads Donnie into the kitchen?

The actors wore these little lights attached to their chests. The liquid spears were then tracked to the actors' movements. This became much more complicated when the camera needed to pan or track with an actor. There was a specific design to the spears with respect to each character. Each one was meant to have its own personality. Donnie's spear becomes alarmed when it realises that its host can see it. It begins to taunt him up the stairs. For me the whole effect is either really funny or very disturbing. I go crazy thinking about what it could imply.

Was it difficult incorporating those digital shots into the film during post-production?

There were always nay-sayers who kept telling me it wasn't going to work, that it would look stupid. I replied to their argument by show-ing them footage from Peter Jackson's *Heavenly Creatures*. There you saw digital effects that came from a character's dementia. The effects were scary because Kate Winslet and Melanie Lynskey reacted to them so well. Thankfully, Jake made the effects work. The digital effects in *Donnie Darko* are specific to the story. We knew that we were trying to do a Salvador Dali comic book. Some people say that it's just a film-school homage to *The Abyss*. To be honest, I just couldn't think

Left: the water barrier.
Below: the metaphysical barrier.

of a better way to illustrate the metaphysical idea of predestination and I wanted to link it with the water barrier in the bathroom scenes. I'm not sure that I will use digital effects again unless a character is confronting some sort of dementia. My rule with digital is: only use it when it's absolutely necessary.

You have mentioned that when you were conceiving this film you were influenced by a video football game.

American football commentator John Madden has this tool that lets him draw on the television screen when they replay the last down during a game. He draws lines on the screen showing exactly what is going to happen, where the players are going to move. I believe that it is called CBS Chalkboard. That inspired the scene where the spears grow out of Donnie's chest. I thought, 'What if there is some John Madden up there in the cosmos who hits the pause button and draws lines telling us where to go?' I thought about that and what kind of Pandora's Box it opens up in terms of ideas. You can think about it for hours, and I did think about it for hours and the only way to stop thinking about it was to write it into the film as a metaphysical element.

Can you tell me something about The Philosophy of Time Travel?

We were getting ready to put the film out in the theatres and there was a lot of anxiety: the anxiety of September 11th, the anxiety of the film not having any marketing budget, not being ready for release, of it disappearing in a couple of weeks and me just wanting to be done with it. I felt like I needed to solve the riddle in my own way as a form of release. It was a way for me to answer all the questions outside of the film. I did not want to do it inside the film for reasons I have already discussed. But at the same time I felt like it was a way for me to come to terms with this mystery I had created. Writing those pages was a way for me to say, 'Here's my theory, I may be wrong, but here it is.' I considered myself to be just a viewer when I wrote it, not the filmmaker. It was meant to be an argument that people could agree or disagree with. Ultimately, I think those pages probably caused people to ask more questions about what it all means.

How many drafts of the screenplay did you go through before you showed it to Sean McKittrick?

Probably two before I showed it to Sean, then we went through two more where we got the length down to 128 pages. When I showed it to Sean it was about 140. My scripts tend to run long, but as I have become more experienced I have found a rhythm to the way I write. I have found a way to be editorial as I write instead of doing it when I finish a draft. So now when I am finished with a first draft, it feels more like a third draft.

Were you surprised that CAA wanted to sign you as a client after reading the screenplay?

My jaw was on the floor. I got a call from two agents named John Campisi and Rob Paris. It came out of nowhere. I thought maybe I would find an attorney somewhere who might want to hip-pocket me. I had no idea I would get signed by the biggest, most powerful talent agency in Hollywood. That came out of nowhere. That was probably my most life-changing moment because people wouldn't have read the script if it did not have this agency stamp on the cover. It's easier to win the lottery than to have someone read your screenplay in Hollywood.

Do you think it really helps having an agent in your corner, building your persona?

This town is built on hype, and on people's fear of missing out on something. If a powerful agent endorses you, it means something. Ultimately, it's about the work, it's the screenplay that matters. But to get them to read it, you need someone who can create a sense of urgency around your screenplay. That is invaluable in getting a film made. The puppeteers positioning your material in such a way that people will throw some cash down on the table and let you do it.

You made the rounds with the script at the Hollywood studios. Can you tell me something about what the reactions were to the script?

Some people were genuinely fascinated by it and genuinely wanted to see the film get made. There were other people who were told that they should be interested in it because other people were interested in it, that they should meet with me because other people were meeting with me. These people didn't understand it, thought it was unproducible, thought I was smoking crack because I was demanding that I direct it. So there was legitimate, sincere interest and there were those who just met me to say they had met me.

You spent a year pitching this project. Did you find a lot of that time wasted in meetings like that?

Oh yeah. There are a lot of meetings where you have a development executive just nodding their head and blowing smoke up your ass. They've forgotten about you thirty seconds before you walk out the door.

Did you find that frustrating?

When you have no evidence, when you have not made a film yet, they have no reason to take you seriously. People can be very condescending towards first-time directors or aspiring directors. It's a tough town and you have to position yourself and articulate yourself very clearly with a sense of confidence, otherwise they are never going to give you that chance. People's condescension and rejection made me angry and frustrated but the anger and frustration made me more determined. This determination ended up giving me confidence because I wanted to prove them all wrong.

As a defence mechanism, you said you developed a sense of arrogance. Was this posture useful?

You have to be careful about being too arrogant because you can turn into an asshole very quickly. It is more about being confident. But confidence can become arrogance very quickly and you have to be very careful about that. You can't direct a film unless you can have a commanding presence on a set; otherwise people are going to take advantage of you. There are a lot of backseat drivers who are ready to come in and tell you how to do your job. That happens a lot with first-time directors – they start to drown and it becomes a runaway train. So from Day One you have to position yourself as the person in charge. When you are twenty-five years old and you have never made a film before, you have to be very careful about that because you can come off as a prima donna, a real asshole.

It sounds like there was quite a bit of showmanship involved in selling your vision of this film. How did you and Sean prepare yourself for these pitching sessions?

Pitching to me is just really obnoxious. I hate the word 'pitch'. It has nothing to do with being an artist. You don't need to know how to sell yourself to be a good artist, but it is a necessary evil. You have to go in there and articulate your ideas clearly and answer every question they throw at you. A lot of people realise when someone is just a good salesman and that is it, it doesn't go any further than that. I think that if you razzle-dazzle them in the room too much, it can be a smoke-screen hiding the fact that there is nothing there. If you are a little awkward, a little disorganised, a little meandering in your 'pitch' of how you are going to direct a film, I wouldn't worry too much, as long as you are being honest. I think that people place far too much emphasis on wowing people in the room. It's become like an episode of *American Idol*.

So how did you 'razzle-dazzle' the studio execs?

I would explain to them the style, the tone of the film, how I'd like to cast it, how it's going to be photographed. You become very schooled in it and it becomes easier to do the more meetings you take. Some-times I would walk in the room with Sean and immediately the meeting would end right there because they were expecting Tim Burton and instead they would get this *Dawson's Creek* reject. They would just say, 'Forget it. It's not going to happen. You're too young. You don't look like a director.' You just deal with it. You move on and go to the next meeting.

Knowing that the studios rarely give money to a first-time director, were you worried about alienating yourself with this kind of confident posture?

No, because it was the only card I had. The only card I had was this script that people really liked and I owned it and I wouldn't sell it. They wanted to take it away from me and I wouldn't let them. After a while they started to think, 'Maybe he really can do it. He's holding out this long. Maybe he really does know what do with it.' Eventually, Drew Barrymore signed on and that was the endorsement that they needed.

After a year of pitching Donnie Darko *it was considered dead around town. But then Jason Schwartzman, the star of* Rushmore, *became attached. How did this happen?*

The script had been copied hundreds of times and had been passed around. It was a script that everyone was reading as a writing sample and it was of interest to a lot of people. Actors were now starting to read it out of curiosity. We heard through the grapevine that Jason liked it and asked about it through his agent. But around town agents were told the project was dead. Development executives love to declare a project dead. But really it was still there, waiting to be made; I still wanted to make it. So we got a meeting with Jason and he told us he wanted to do it and he became attached to it, and all of a sudden people came out of the woodwork, it was alive again. The excitement started to build, and all of sudden we had an offer from Pandora to make the film for $2.5 million. During this time Jason's agent Sharon Sheinwold, who was incredibly supportive, sent it to Nancy Juvonen at Flower Films. Nancy read it on the plane going to Las Vegas, flipped out, gave it to Drew, and they both accosted my agent at ShoWest, telling him that they wanted to be involved and help get it made. My agent then called me and told me the news and I asked for a meeting with them. Two days later Sean and I drove down to the set of *Charlie's Angels* and we were there in the trailer with Drew, her dogs and Nancy. I asked her to play the English teacher who gets fired and she said she would love to if we would let her production company help produce the film. We shook hands and then before we knew it the budget was up to $4.5 million, which was what we really needed to make the film. It was fantasyland.

Can you tell me something about that meeting with Drew Barrymore, what your expectations were?

I never get nervous when I meet celebrities, but with Drew it was a different story. We're the same age but really we're not. She's lived a lot more life than I have. In person, she is the most approachable and endearing woman you could ever meet. To think that she would be a mentor and godmother to this project seemed like a poetic fit. It seemed like the stars were aligned.

Because of your fondness for E.T.*?*

There was just something about her and what she had been through in her life that just made her the right mentor for this project. I think she and Nancy had had those meetings too where they walked into a meeting and said, 'We're producers,' and people just rolled their eyes. I think they identified with our struggle to be taken seriously. They were willing to roll the dice on me and on Sean. Other more established producers were unwilling to do that; they were very sceptical and unwilling to stick their necks out.

Richard Kelly with Drew Barrymore.

Drew Barrymore in *E.T.*

How did your director of photography, Steven Poster, get involved?

We were looking through a stack of résumés and I noticed that he had shot a Ridley Scott film, *Someone to Watch Over Me*. I was stupefied to learn that we could afford someone who had shot a Ridley Scott film. Once you shoot a Ridley Scott film, you can retire, you've made it. Steven hadn't shot a film in two years; he'd been doing commercials and music videos. I met with Steven and the first thing he said to me was, 'I want you to know two things. First, I want you to forget about the age difference between us. Second, I don't ever want to be a director so don't worry, I won't try and take this film away from you.' Which put my mind at ease, so I begged him to take the job, cut his price and work on the film. It was an amazing collaborative experience. He got us anamorphic lenses. Very few filmmakers get to use anamorphic lenses on their first film because they are expensive and difficult to use in terms of the amount of time it takes to light for them. We were granted luxuries because of Steven Poster: because of his reputation, his crew and his relationship with Panavision. He got us an unprecedented amount of equipment for very little money and got Panavision to cut us an amazing deal. He's the reason the film looks the way it does.

Was CAA helpful in securing your talented and well-known cast?

When Drew signed on it became something that everyone wanted to be a part of. She agreed to do the movie for scale. That set a precedent for all the other actors who wanted to be a part of it.

Once Jake Gyllenhaal signed on to do the movie, you met for a month of script meetings. What did you two work on at those meetings?

Jake comes from a family of filmmakers. I love it when an actor comes to me with very specific notes on a character. That means they are invested in it, they are making it their own by digesting it. He'd come over to my house and he would have written a bunch of notes on his script and we would debate and negotiate how we wanted to adjust every line. Maybe other directors look at that as being a nightmarish experience, having an actor come in and do a polish on the script, but I was fine with it. It helped his performance and I'll probably do that again on my next film with the lead actor.

Can you tell me something about your strategy in pre-production for the design of the film? It has a very specific look with its formal compositions and intricate set pieces.

I showed my crew several films. As a lighting reference I showed them Francis Ford Coppola's *Peggy Sue Got Married*, which was shot by the late Jordan Cronenweth. His work in the prom sequence has an idealised nostalgia, a polished, burnished nostalgia, which I wanted to emulate for a lot of the night sequences, both interior and exterior. Also, Kathleen Turner's prom dress – I wanted to use a similar costuming for the dancers in Sparkle Motion. I wanted there to be a Norman Rockwell feeling to Middlesex and I felt Cronenweth captured a Norman Rockwell feeling in that film. As a tonal reference we looked at Kubrick's *Lolita*. The absurdism of that film. We lifted a few things: recreating Vivian Darkbloom's outfit for Maggie Gyllenhaal at the Halloween party; the footlights in the Sparkle Motion performance were taken from Lolita's play. The tone of that film was similar to what

Peggy Sue (Kathleen Turner) in her prom dress, from *Peggy Sue Got Married.*

I was trying to establish in *Donnie Darko* – its absurdist humour and pathos.

You didn't storyboard until after you saw the locations?

You can do a certain amount of storyboarding but you can't accurately storyboard the film until you lock every location. When we got our locations we went on an early tech scout and I took hundreds of photographs from every angle. Then I picked photographs from the angles we wanted to use and I gave them to a storyboard artist. It made them more accurate.

It's interesting that you used a professional when you are such an experienced illustrator yourself.

I couldn't draw them because I would spend an hour on each one. It would have been a waste of time. I would start shading in everything, adding shadow, and it would have become really tedious.

Can you tell me something about the first day of shooting?

Steven Poster and Richard Kelly on the first day of shooting
in the San Angeles Crest Mountains.

It was the first shot of the movie on the cliff. The sun had just come up and it was amazing. It was a pre-production photography day so we only had to get that shot and the mist where Donnie stands up and a couple of background plate shots. So it was literally a two-hour shoot then we went home. It was heaven. It was so wonderful. On top of the world at dawn and I had just directed the first shot of my first film. Jake and I had two bikes and we were riding around like kids. Then we were off on the adventure of principal photography.

Filming lasted exactly twenty-eight days. Did you feel that you were getting everything you needed or was the shoot moving too fast?

It was a train that took off and wouldn't stop. We were just trying to keep up. We were staying on schedule by the skin of our teeth every single day. It was relentless. We were constantly juggling things, working with Tom Hayslip, our line producer, who pulled off miracles for us: locations, schedules, budgets.

Having not had much experience with professional actors, were you worried that they would not respond to your direction?

I think I put them at ease, up front, by saying, 'I have no idea of what I am doing. I don't know how I am supposed to talk to you, so I am just going to talk to you like you are my friends.' I knew exactly what I wanted the characters to be like, I knew who they were, developing a pretty interesting backstory for each one. For example, I said to Noah Wyle, 'This is who I think Professor Monnitoff is: he went to MIT, he worked for the government for a little while, he decided he wanted to be a science teacher, he smokes pot, he's diabetic, he loves to play video games, he's screwing Ms Pomeroy and they have this thing going on.' And Noah said, 'I get it.' It was all I knew how to do. I think a lot of first-time directors make the mistake of overdoing it and trying to come up with some flowery method dialogue. If you just keep it as simple as you can, the actors will respond to it. It helps if you are the writer too.

Why? Because it's in your bones?

Yes. Having written the screenplay yourself is half the battle of communicating with your actors because you have had to make decisions about the details of those characters' lives in the writing process. The characters come from you.

During production you gave Drew Barrymore a few notes that helped with her performance, such as telling her only to smile once during her performance. Can you tell me something about that story and why it helped her re-think her character?

Drew came to the set straight off of *Charlie's Angels* and we really had no time to rehearse with her. My thing with Drew was to try and get her to play her character as someone who is irrational and somewhat immature. A teacher who has yet to have her spirit destroyed, but is on her way out. She doesn't realise the repercussions of what she's doing, an example of this is the way she taunts the kids. It was a conscious decision for Drew not to play the cutie-pie in this movie. Her character is feeling these bizarre impulses: she's manipulating the kids right off the bat, she's humiliating the kids, trying to put Donnie and Gretchen together. Some people don't want Drew to play anything else but the cutie-pie. It's this monkey on her back from her days as a child actor and it's not fair to pigeonhole her that way because she is capable of so much more.

Can you describe, technically speaking, how you designed the sequence when Donnie arrives at school and we are introduced to all the major characters in the story? The camerawork, the choreographed move-ment of the actors, the music chosen . . . it is a very effective sequence.

The sequence was originally intended to be a single tracking shot, but the location was so big that it became logistically impossible; as a result we divided it into four segments. It was choreographed to intro-duce all of the major characters from the school part of the movie, just as we introduced the family earlier in the film with the Echo and The Bunnymen song, and was to be our second 'musical number'. It fore-shadows the chain of events, this microcosm of the entire story that is about to unfold.

To efficiently introduce the characters I wanted each actor to be doing something emblematic of their character. The goal was for the audience to understand exactly who these people are without a single line of dialogue. I asked myself, how could we capture the essence of a character in a single moment? Steven Poster pre-rigged the school so that we could have a 360-degree shooting environment. I was hiding with him in one of the classrooms, calling out the camera speed changes to the first AC who along with the Steadicam operator, was the only crewmember in the school hallway. It was a live set; the actors could go anywhere and do anything I wanted them to do. All of the slow-motion pieces were created in camera because I really don't care for optical slow motion. It would have been inappropriate for the rhythm of the Tears for Fears song. The fast-motion segments were all done optically except for when we fly through the window into Drew's classroom. That one was in camera. I knew it would end with the lyric 'time flies'. My editor Sam Bauer had to cut the song very carefully so that you don't realise that there is about two minutes of it missing.

Can you remember one moment in the editing of the film that really pleased and surprised you? How cutting two bits together made a major impact on you?

I remember we actually shot footage of Donnie telling Kitty Farmer to shove the Lifeline exercise card up her ass. She gave him this look of terror and outrage, turns to the class and says, 'Excuse me!' and walks out. It was hilarious. However, in the editing room I realised that the laugh was going to be so much bigger if we cut out early, straight to the Principal's office. You're left wondering what he said, milking the joke for a little longer. When Kitty repeats it back in front of the parents and the dad laughs, it became three times funnier than it would have been if you saw Donnie tell her to her face. In the end everything comes back to creating suspense. Even comedy is about creating suspense for the punch line.

What was the major conflict with the financiers during post-production? Can you tell me why you fought so hard for it?

I don't want to dwell so much on the conflict during post-production. It happens on every film. I think that when you have a first-time director – and everyone realises that the film could be something really special – everyone wants to throw in his or her two cents. This was the kind of film where everyone had a specific and very passionate opinion about something within the story that they thought was necessary or unnecessary.

But the story was so fragile that I had to fight like hell to keep it from falling apart. Editing was like playing a game of Jenga only with porcelain blocks and no beer. That's not a lot of fun. If you pulled out this therapist scene, or that school scene, the plot would have fallen to pieces. Sometimes I had to scream and yell and sometimes I was right and sometimes I was wrong. Sometimes people were making horrible suggestions, other times I was being a stubborn, self-indulgent director on the verge of a nervous breakdown.

Judging from the jovial nature of the DVD cast and crew commentary, it sounded like everyone had a good time making this film. Did you do anything, as a director, to engender a certain spirit of togetherness among the cast and crew while working?

I think when everyone is there for no money, you are there because you love the material; you're not there for a paycheck. So right away there is a democracy, an idea that everyone is on equal terms. That engenders a community spirit. I think actors have a really good time on independent films. I think studio films can be slow and tedious. It's about getting paid, a lot of people are not so happy with the script. It's about paying the mortgage on their house; it's about positioning themselves for their career. When you are doing an independent film you are there because you love a script. You can see the fire in the performer's eye, I don't know if you see that in a big studio film.

The budget came in at $4.5 million. You said you owe a lot of people favours for helping you on the film. Who were these people and what roles did they play in helping the film stay under control, financially?

Steven Poster got us every discount in the book: lighting, grip, electric, and camera. Everything came at a tremendous discount; he even got his crew to cut his price. Tom Hayslip, the line producer, worked miracles with the budget. Sean McKittrick was incredibly organised, so on-the-game as a producer. He helped me get what I needed and what I wanted, which was essential because I am so disorganised. Alexander Hammond, our production designer, built his own sets for very little money and found a jet engine in Arizona. April Ferry, the costume designer, worked miracles for us. My friend Kelly Carlton did the water barrier effects for $5000. The whole crew was incredibly generous.

Was the film profitable?

Domestically it only made half a million dollars, but worldwide it turned a profit, thanks to a good theatrical run in the UK. The Region 1 DVD sold very well, although that process was something of a nightmare. When a movie fails at the box-office, the home video people come out of the woodwork. The company that was in charge of the DVD, a bottom-feeder house called Silver Nitrate Home Video, they were insistent on re-packaging it as a teen-slasher film. I had quite a war with them. I remember at the first meeting sitting across from this marketing woman at a restaurant, and she was explaining to me that we needed to remove Mary McDonnell and Katharine Ross from the above-the-title block, because teenagers didn't care about them. These are two women who have been nominated for multiple academy awards; they did this movie for scale! This idiot wants to remove their names because she thinks it will help sales. It was such an idiotic and insulting display of ageism against Mary and Katharine. I wanted to take my beer and dump it over her head.

I was walking down the road in London before the film was released and there was this restaurant that jutted out towards the road, exposing a broad, cream-coloured wall. It was an empty canvas for a graffiti artist. On that wall was spray-painted, in tall block letters, the words DONNIE DARKO.

Yeah, there was graffiti art all over London. Tom Grievson at Metro-dome showed it to a bunch of the top graffiti artists in London and

'There was graffiti all over London.'

I guess they all flipped out for it. It became this renegade campaign; the graffiti artists took it upon themselves to promote our movie. It was very flattering. They did an amazing art exhibit too. I never thought I'd see a Smurf orgy on canvas, but I now have.

The score by Michael Andrews was very effective. How did your collaboration come about?

For some reason a lot of directors keep going back to the same five guys to compose their films. I was never going to be able to afford one of those five superstars so I decided to find a genius that had not had the opportunity to show his stuff. Jim Juvonen, Nancy's younger brother, called me up and told me about this guy living down in San Diego. We met and hit it off. When we were close to locking the picture, I was in there almost every day with Michael, working out the score. The score was recorded over the period of about a month. He was influenced by Jerry Goldsmith and his scores from the seventies. Mike also has stacks and stacks of obscure records that also helped, a lot of stuff I had never heard of. I mean, he'll go on to eBay and buy a flute from eighteenth-century Russia. He's all about finding unusual ways to create music. He created that score from scratch, for no money.

You have said that there is a lot of armchair quarterbacking that goes on with first-time directors, especially in the editing room. How did this manifest itself in post-production and how did you handle it?

It got frustrating because when there is a film that is open-ended and it's lacking a certain amount of closure, by design, there is always going to be an inspired debate about the length of the film and what you don't cut. As a first-time director I found it a little frustrating sometimes. Sometimes it becomes very confrontational and upsetting but you know that this is your one shot to make your film. In ten years no one is going to remember that you yelled at your financier because they wanted you to cut something, they're going to remember what's in the film. So if I have to yell at someone I will. And I won almost every battle. I probably let it get to me too much and I lost sleep, lost weight and became this insane maniac for several months. It was an unpleasant time, but I got through it.

You have said that if you could change anything about your experience on the film you would have 'stressed less and not taken it so seriously. I wish I'd just calmed the fuck down a little bit.' Was it the financial responsibilities making you so stressed?

It was two things: getting the final cut of the film the way I wanted it and then, even more so, selling the film to a distributor and having them not re-cut it against my wishes. That is the nightmare of any filmmaker who brings a film to the Sundance Film Festival. You have to get in there and fight. You run the risk of alienating the distributor or getting a bad reputation around town, but you know what? No one is going to remember that if your movie is good and it gets good reviews or makes money. It's personal, it's your art and they are going to take it away from you. I'm speaking in general terms, because Newmarket was very good to me; they were the only ones who wanted to distribute the film. However, most distributors have a complete lack of respect for the director and his or her vision.

There was a lot of buzz at Sundance surrounding Donnie Darko. *How did that affect the sale of your film to potential distributors?*

Buzz is the most obnoxious thing; it is truly horrible for your film, especially at Sundance. If you come into Sundance with buzz – and I hate that word, with a passion – immediately people are going to be sharpening their knives.

Why do you think that is?

That's just the way it is. People are looking for a reason to shoot something down. Also, I think if you show up at Sundance with a movie with visual effects, Drew Barrymore and a big cast, there will be a lot of people who will be sceptical and derisive of it because they don't think it's really an independent film. That's one part of the Sundance reaction. Others were overwhelmingly excited that it was there and acknowledged it as being an independent film. But almost because of the fact that it looked like it cost a lot more than it did – and because of the visual effects – there were a lot of people who immediately thought it was a disingenuous commercial enterprise invading the sacred independent scene. Sundance is great, but it has been getting a little more corporate every year and perhaps there is a backlash against anything that is seen as being corporate or commercial. For some reason people thought of *Donnie Darko* as being something that didn't belong in competition at Sundance. It was touted as the first film in competition at Sundance with significant digital effects. I think that bothered a certain old-school way of thinking. They want to see the movie about lesbians making fudge. I love lesbians . . . and I love fudge . . . but I don't necessarily want to see that film . . . shot digitally of course. Programming director Geoffrey Gilmore was really supportive of the film. He knew that it belonged there.

How did the first screening with an audience go?

We had never shown it to a theatre full of people. I was pretty relaxed before the screening and I was very content with the film we made. I knew there was still some work to do, I knew it was still running a little long here or there, but I felt really content. I just wanted someone to buy it so we could get it out there in the theatres. It was great seeing it with an audience. I was just relieved that they were laughing . . . in the right places.

How did you feel when the festival ended and there was no deal in place?

It was frustrating because of the hype around the film. Immediately the distributors wanted to dismiss it as being something that didn't work. A lot of the distributors bad-mouthed the film as soon as they walked out of the screening. They do that to discourage competition from other buyers. The acquisition executives will talk shit about films – even ones that they like – to keep someone else from getting something that they might be interested in. There's a lot of jockeying and hearsay that goes into selling your film at Sundance and it is just nauseating. It makes you want to puke. *Entertainment Weekly* does this thing called the Buzz-o-Meter. They actually put the buzz for your film on a chart. Of course we started off-the-charts high . . . then bottomed out when no deal was in place. There was nowhere to go but down. People read something like that and almost immediately the film is considered to be a failure around town. No one wants to touch it. I cut the Buzz-o-Meter out of the magazine and put it on my bulletin board so I could chart the buzz throughout the remainder of my life on earth.

I never, ever, want to make a film again that doesn't have a domestic distributor before we start shooting. You lose sleep and you're at the mercy of acquisitions executives. They have an opinion, then they go back on their opinion, they kiss your ass one day then talk shit about your film the next day. It's all too much.

Ironically . . . Lisa Schwarzbaum at *Entertainment Weekly* gave the film an A– when it was released. The same grade I got for *The Vomiteer* in college. Perhaps I will remake *The Vomiteer* and bring it to Sundance. I can hand out barf bags.

How do you feel about the way the movie was received on its theatrical release in the States and abroad?

I was just thrilled that it got released, period. There were about four months when it was going to get dumped onto pay cable or home video. It was very close to not getting a theatrical release because distributors felt it was not marketable. Newmarket was the only distributor who was still interested. But at that point there was an offer from a cable company where the financiers could have made more money, up front, dumping it onto cable. I was in there begging, telling them that I would write a free script if they gave my movie a theatrical release. I was willing to chop off my arm to get it in theatres. I think I actually did offer to chop off my arm.

They probably would have preferred the free script.

Actually, they probably would have preferred to see me chop off my arm. I knew that if it did not get a theatrical release it would be the end of my career. I would have to go find something else to do for a living, especially after the hype of Sundance. If it goes straight-to-video after that much attention, then the film and the filmmaker are considered a failure. When they finally said they were going to put it out on Halloween, I was so thankful. As long as they put it on one screen, for one weekend, I could avoid the curse of the straight-to-video tag. A lot of good films get dumped onto video and a lot of films that don't deserve a theatrical release, get one. It's not really a fair assessment of quality, by any means. So when September 11th happened we lost a month and a half of publicity, theatre booking time; everything got thrown out of whack and literally there was no publicity. I think they made a bad decision in putting it in eight cities. It played very well in LA and New York, but the theatres were empty in Washington, DC, Chicago and Seattle. It died the opening weekend as a result. So they pulled all the newspaper ads, all the marketing and it was left to linger in LA and New York for a few months, then it just disappeared. You can't recover from an opening weekend like that. If they had just put it in two theatres in LA and two theatres in New

York and let it build, it would have played much better. But it's OK; it got released.

And you still have your arm.

Yes, I still have my arm and I have a career. I would have been so upset for all the people who worked on this film for no money had it not been given a theatrical release.

Philip French, writing in the London Sunday paper, The Observer, *noted that Graham Greene's 'The Destructors' argued that destruction is a form of creation. In light of your film being released so soon after 9/11, were you worried about the parallels?*

I think any time your art takes on new meaning after a cataclysmic event there is nothing you can do because perception has changed. You can only hope that it is not going to offend people or upset them any more than they already are. You hope it is not going to pour gasoline on a fire that already exists in people's lives. We thought about it for a few days and decided that it if there was a resonance about the film then we hoped it would somehow be cathartic for people instead of upsetting them. I think the film was received favourably in light of 9/11. It did not offend people.

Why do you think Donnie Darko *polarised so many film critics?*

I think it might be a generational thing. There are people who remember the eighties the way it was in the film. There are other people remember the eighties as something out of a Bret Easton Ellis novel, hanging out in clubs in New York City. I remember the John Hughes version of the eighties. I think some critics just didn't know what to do with it. They weren't open to experiencing the film with their guard down, letting it be what it was. They wanted to tag it as something and because they couldn't tag it as something they said it was muddled, pretentious – or they'd say something like, 'He's just young. He's trying to do too much.' We got some really good reviews but we got some people who also said it was adolescent nonsense. You are going to get that from people who are not willing to engage in the film, look at it more than once. Although the people who were supportive of it were very passionate about it.

1

The film ignited a lot of interpretation chatter on the Internet. What did you make of some of these readings, such as Donnie being the messiah?

Whoa. It's a comic-book story in a way and he is a kind of superhero. I think there is a messiah undercurrent to a lot of superhero stories. Any time you are dealing with a hero who has to save the world there is going to be a link to Christ mythology. You know we made a sight gag as a reference to Scorsese's film: when Donnie comes out of the cinema the marquee shows *The Last Temptation of Christ*.

What about some of the other stuff on the Internet? Do you follow any of it?

I've seen some of the fan sites. It's pretty amazing. I had no idea that a couple of years later people would be talking about it. It's rewarding and flattering and it just makes me more determined not to sell out and to keep doing stuff like this.

You have said that, 'No matter how successful or unsuccessful I am in my career I think I'll always have that underdog mentality.' Now that you've made your first film, with Drew Barrymore, when you were twenty-five, do you really think of yourself as an underdog?

What I was trying to say was I would try my hardest not to sell out, not to make a film for purely mercenary purposes, especially if the studio thinks it is a safe bet. In that sense, you're an underdog in getting the studio to take a risk. The material might not work, might not be palatable to an audience, it might not sell, so who knows, maybe in five years time I'll be directing some really horrible romantic comedy.

Have you felt any notions of resentment from others in the filmmaking community who resent that your first feature was produced so successfully?

There's always going to be resentment and I probably deserve it. I think I definitely got very lucky, getting a lot of opportunities afforded to me at a very young age. I'm just trying to do good work and not screw it up. They probably would have resented me more had I got all these opportunities and made something that sucked. The only way I can say thank you for all these opportunities is to make a good film

li

and to help out, to help other filmmakers make good films. That is the way you give back.

What are you working on now?

I'm going to do a science-fiction film called *Knowing*.

Can you tell us something about Knowing?

I can't comment on the next one. I don't comment until the first day of shooting. Nothing is real until film is rolling.

You have said that your be-all, end-all dream is to meet Steven Spielberg. Why?

He's the king. Meeting Spielberg would be pretty amazing. Maybe one day, maybe one day . . .

Venice Beach, California, 13 March 2003

DONNIE DARKO

This is the shooting script that was used
by the cast and crew during the shooting of the film

Fade in:

EXT. CARPATHIAN RIDGE – DAWN (SATURDAY, 5 AM)

We descend upon Carpathian Ridge, a crescent-shaped cliff that extrudes from the dense Virginia evergreens above a deep rock canyon. The cliff marks the end of a dirt road that winds down from above.

Donnie Darko (sixteen) is asleep at the edge of the cliff. With his bike collapsed next to him, he is shivering, curled up in the foetal position.

He slowly opens his eyes and looks around, disoriented by the morning light. He then stands up, looking down into the expansive rock canyon. After a moment of hesitation, he takes his bike back up the hill.

EXT. MIDDLESEX – MORNING (11 AM)

Montage is choreographed to 'Never Tear Us Apart' by INXS.

Donnie pedals down into the suburban village of Middlesex, Virginia . . . passing by a large rock 'Middlesex' rock-pattern.

Donnie pedals past two neighbourhood women who are speedwalking with handweights. They smile at him.

A Pontiac Trans-Am speeds by.

EXT. NEIGHBOURHOOD STREET – DAY (SATURDAY, 1 PM)

Donnie turns the corner and heads towards the garage.

We pan over to the Darko house . . . moving through the front yard where Eddie Darko (forty-four) pulls the cord and his gas-powered leaf-blower roars to life.

Elizabeth Darko (nineteen) comes out the front door. She approaches her dad from behind. Eddie turns and aims the leaf-blower at her face . . . blasting her with air.

EXT. DARKO DRIVEWAY — NEXT

Donnie parks his bike and goes inside.

EXT. DARKO BACKYARD/PATIO — NEXT

We pull back from Samantha Darko (ten) as she is jumping on a trampoline and pan over to Rose Darko (forty-two) as she sits at a table reading a paperback copy of Stephen King's It. *She glances over to the kitchen.*

INT. KITCHEN — NEXT

Donnie walks into the kitchen. He then goes to the refrigerator. Printed in magic marker on the refrigerator notepad is the phrase: WHERE IS DONNIE?

INT. FAMILY ROOM — EVENING (5 PM)

The opening theme of 'Who's the Boss?' begins as we see Tony Danza's blue van and the title card. We reveal Samantha, sitting on the floor, singing softly to the theme song 'Brand New Life' performed by Larry Weiss.

We pan over to Donnie, sitting in the La-Z-Boy.

INT. KITCHEN — EVENING (6 PM)

The Darko family has convened for dinner. They eat silently for several moments.

ELIZABETH
I'm voting for Dukakis.

EDDIE
Perhaps when you have children of your own that need braces, and you can't afford them because half of your husband's paycheck goes to the federal government, you'll regret that decision.

ELIZABETH
(amused bitterness)
I'm not gonna squeeze one out until I'm thirty.

4

DONNIE

Will you still be working at Yarn Barn? 'Cause that's a great place to raise children.

ROSE

No, a year of partying is enough. She'll be going to Harvard this fall.

ELIZABETH

I haven't been accepted yet, Mother.

ROSE
(smiles)

If you think Michael Dukakis will provide for this country prior to the point when you decide to squeeze one out, then I think you're misinformed.

SAMANTHA

When can I squeeze one out?

DONNIE
(to his sister)

Not until like . . . eighth grade.

ROSE
(to Donnie)

Excuse me?

ELIZABETH

Donnie? You're a dick.

DONNIE

Whoa, Elizabeth. A little hostile there. Maybe you should be the one in therapy. Then Mom and Dad can pay someone two hundred dollars an hour to listen to all of your thoughts . . . so we won't have to.

ELIZABETH

Maybe you'd like to tell Mom and Dad why you stopped taking your medication.

An awkward silence.

ROSE
(surprised)

You stopped taking your medication?

SAMANTHA

When can I squeeze one out, Mom?

DONNIE
(*glaring at Elizabeth*)

You're such a fuck-ass.

ROSE

When did you stop taking your medication?

ELIZABETH
(*laughing*)

Did you just call me a fuck-ass?

ROSE

That's enough.

ELIZABETH
(*to Donnie*)

You can suck a fuck.

DONNIE

Oh, please tell me, Elizabeth, how exactly does one suck a fuck?

ROSE
(*disgusted*)

We will not have this kind of language at the dinner table.

They are silent for a moment.

SAMANTHA

What's a fuck-ass?

Despite his brave efforts to hold back laughter, Eddie Darko lets out a slight guffaw.

INT. ELIZABETH'S ROOM – EVENING (SATURDAY NIGHT, 9 PM)

Elizabeth talks on the phone, getting ready for her Saturday night. Rose knocks and then enters.

ELIZABETH
(*into the phone*)

No. I took a year off to be with you. (*Beat.*) Of course I care. Don't get angry. (*covering the phone*) What?

                              ROSE
How did you know –

                           ELIZABETH
                         (cutting her off)
I didn't realise that it was such a big deal.

                              ROSE
It is a big deal.

                           ELIZABETH
I caught him flushing pills down the toilet. He knows you
check the container.

INT. DONNIE'S ROOM – NEXT

Donnie lies on his bed, reading Collected Short Stories *by Graham
Greene. His room is an organised wreck.*

Rose enters and begins to pick things up off the floor.

                             DONNIE
Get out of my room.

Rose bitterly turns to leave, but stops at the door.

                              ROSE
I wish I knew where you went at night. (*Beat.*) Did you toilet
paper the Johnson's house?

                             DONNIE
                         (*still reading*)
I stopped rolling houses in the sixth grade, Mom. (*Beat.*) Get
out of my room.

                              ROSE
You know . . . it would be nice to look at you some time . . .
and see my son. I don't recognise this person today.

                             DONNIE
Then why don't you start taking the goddamn pills?

*Donnie leans over and turns off his lamp. Rose turns and leaves her
son alone in the dark, closing the door behind her.*

Bitch.

INT. UPSTAIRS HALLWAY — NEXT

Rose stops in her tracks, hearing this. She then walks into her bedroom and closes the door.

INT. MASTER BEDROOM — NEXT

Rose gets into bed with Eddie, who is reading a hardback copy of Stephen King's The Tommyknockers.

> ROSE
> Our son just called me a bitch.

> EDDIE
> *(beat)*
> You're not a bitch.

INT. UPSTAIRS BATHROOM — NEXT

He removes his pills from the medicine cabinet. We see insert that reads: L. THURMAN M.D.

He looks at the bottle for a moment, and then takes three pills and swallows them . . . staring at his reflection in the mirror.

INT. MASTER BEDROOM — NIGHT (12 AM)

Eddie sits up in bed, unable to sleep.

INT. FAMILY ROOM — NEXT

The TV pops on. Eddie drops into the La-Z-Boy.

They are replaying a Bush/Dukakis debate. Eddie laughs.

INT. FOYER — NEXT

We pull back and pan over to a grandfather clock . . . as the hand reaches midnight.

Title card:

OCTOBER 2 1988

INT. DONNIE'S ROOM – NIGHT (EARLY SUNDAY MORNING, I AM)

VOICE
(whisper)

Wake . . . up . . . Donnie.

*Donnie jerks upright in his bed, awakened from a bad dream.
He looks over at his alarm clock: 12.50 a.m. His expression is
distant . . . confused.*

INT. FOYER – NEXT

Donnie walks downstairs.

INT. FAMILY ROOM – NEXT

Donnie stares at Eddie, asleep in the La-Z-Boy.

INT. KITCHEN – NEXT

*Donnie walks into the kitchen, removes the magic marker from the
refrigerator message board.*

INT. FOYER – NEXT

Donnie walks to the front and exits the house.

EXT. DARKO HOUSE, FRONT YARD – NEXT

Donnie walks down the front walk to the street.

EXT. NEIGHBOURHOOD STREET – NEXT

Donnie walks down the street.

EXT. SEVENTH HOLE – NIGHT (1:30 AM)

Donnie arrives next to the pin and stares off into the distance.

9

VOICE

Helluva night for a walk . . . huh, Donnie?

Donnie stares off into the distance.

Tonight is very special, Donnie.

DONNIE

What?

VOICE

I've been watching you. (*Beat.*) Do you believe in God, Donnie?

He doesn't answer. He holds his stomach, taking deep breaths.

God loves his children, Donnie. God loves you.

There . . . standing on the seventh hole is a six-foot-tall figure dressed in a grotesque bunny suit.

Donnie stares at the Bunny nervously as a wave of nausea overcomes him.

BUNNY

My name is Frank. (*Beat.*) I want you to follow me.

DONNIE

Why?

FRANK

I'm here to save you. (*Beat.*) The world is coming to an end, Donnie.

Donnie doesn't answer.

Look up in the sky, Donnie.

He looks up into the black night.

28 days . . . 6 hours . . . 42 minutes . . . 12 seconds. That is when the world will end.

Donnie looks back at Frank. His expression is a vacant expanse of confusion.

INT. FOYER – NIGHT

Elizabeth comes through the front door, leans back against it, closing her eyes.

INT. FAMILY ROOM – NIGHT

Eddie Darko sleeps reclined in the La-Z-Boy. The final notes of the Channel 12 National Anthem fade away to static.

From above . . . a thunderous crash. Plaster rains from the ceiling . . . Books fly off the bookshelf as the entire wall-mount collapses to the floor.

Eddie jerks awake.

INT. FOYER – NEXT

Elizabeth falls back in horror as plaster rains down from around the chandelier . . . debris falling in the dining-room doorway.

EXT. SEVENTH HOLE – MORNING (SUNDAY MORNING, 10 AM)

Donnie is curled up, asleep on the green. A golf ball lands on the green and rolls within inches of his head.

A golf cart filled with four older men arrives. Dr Fisher (forty-five) gets out first.

> DR FISHER
> Donnie Darko? (*Beat.*) Son? What's going on here?

Jim Cunningham (forty), the man riding shotgun, gets out of the cart and walks over.

> JIM CUNNINGHAM
> Who is it, Don?

> DR FISHER
> Eddie Darko's kid.

Donnie gets up and brushes himself off. On his arm he sees something written in black magic marker.

Numbers . . . 28:06:42:12

Donnie stares at the numbers on his arm, confused.

> DR FISHER
> (*to Jim, kissing his ass*)
> Sorry about this, Jim, just a . . . a kid from the neighbourhood. (*back to Donnie*) So let's stay off the greens at night, OK?

Jim Cunningham stares at Donnie with a friendly grin.

> DONNIE
> Sorry, Dr Fisher. It won't happen again.

EXT. NEIGHBOURHOOD STREET/DARKO HOUSE – MORNING (11 AM)

Donnie walks down the street towards his house.

A fire engine. Two police cars. A news van . . . All parked in front of his house.

There are dozens of neighbours in the street surrounding a barricade. Donnie moves through the crowd where a Police Officer is standing.

> DONNIE
> Hey, I live here!

> POLICE OFFICER
> Are you . . . Donnie Darko?

> DONNIE
> Yeah!

The Officer lets him through.

Near the cul-de-sac there is a large caterpillar crane lifting something from inside the house. There are firemen roaming around. Two Police Officers are speaking with Eddie and Rose. Donnie looks over at the house.

A crane lifts a gigantic jet engine over from the house towards a large flatbed truck. Firemen kick pieces of wood and shingle from the roof.

He turns and sees his entire family standing there. Eddie is holding Samantha.

> SAMANTHA
> It fell on your room.

EXT. CUL-DE-SAC – LATER ON

Two men in suits approach from a black sedan. A police officer directs them to Rose. One of the men removes a badge from his pocket and holds it up for Rose to see.

MAN

Ms Darko, my name is Bob Garland and this is David Coleman. We're with the FAA. If you don't mind we'd like to speak with you and your husband privately.

Elizabeth looks over at Donnie with a grin.

ELIZABETH
(*whispering*)
They don't know where it came from.

Donnie looks over in awe as the mammoth engine is now strapped to the flatbed truck. A man in a silver fire suit sprays the engine down with water.

EXT. CUL-DE-SAC – MOMENTS LATER

Eddie is signing some documents in front of Garland at a table that has been set up. Another FAA guy is there.

FAA MAN
(*pointing to the document*)
And then here as well.

Eddie signs off, and Garland takes the documents.

GARLAND
We've arranged for you to stay at a hotel, get some sleep. We'll take care of things here.

Eddie picks Samantha up into his arms. He stands with Rose and Elizabeth . . . turning towards Donnie . . . who seems lost in a trance.

EDDIE
Come on, Donnie . . . we're going to a hotel.

INT. HOLIDAY INN, ROOM 614 – SUNDOWN (SUNDAY NIGHT, 5:30 PM)

Donnie lies in bed, watching television. Elizabeth is spread out on the other bed. Samantha sits on the edge of Elizabeth's bed, holding a stuffed unicorn named Ariel.

SAMANTHA
If it fell from a plane then, what happened to the plane?

ELIZABETH

They don't know, Samantha.

SAMANTHA

Is there any way that we can make money from this? Couldn't we get on television if we sue the airline?

INT. HOLIDAY INN, ROOM 615 – NEXT

Rose and Eddie lie awake in the dark.

ROSE

So let me get this straight. No airline will claim ownership of the engine. So we have to wait for the FAA to decide who fixes my roof. (*Beat.*) Fuck that. We're taking the money out of savings.

EDDIE
(*quoting Rod Serling*)

You are entering a new dimension of sight and sound . . .

Rose begins to laugh.

INT. HOLIDAY INN, ROOM 614 – NEXT

SAMANTHA

Why do I have to sleep with Donnie? He stinks.

DONNIE

When you fall asleep tonight I'm gonna fart in your face.

SAMANTHA
(*walking to the door*)

I'm telling Mom.

ELIZABETH

Samantha, don't go over there.

INT. HOLIDAY INN, ROOM 615 – LATER THAT NIGHT

EDDIE

Frankie Feedler.

ROSE

What?

EDDIE

Frankie Feedler. You remember him from high school?

ROSE

(*long beat*)

He was a year ahead of us?

EDDIE

He died, remember? On the way to the prom. (*Beat.*) He was doomed.

Rose lies there silently.

Jesus Christ. They could have said the same thing about Donnie. Our Donnie. (*Beat.*) But he dodged it. He dodged his bullet, Rose.

Rose rolls over to embrace him.

That's my boy.

Moments later the door to the adjoining room opens. It is Samantha.

SAMANTHA

Mom, Donnie said he's gonna fart in my face.

Title card:

OCTOBER 3 1988

EXT. BUS STOP – MORNING (MONDAY MORNING, 7 AM)

Rose drops Donnie and Samantha off at the corner.

ROSE

Ms Farmer will pick you up from recital. Bye, now.

She pulls off in the Taurus.

Already waiting at the bus stop is Joanie James (eleven). Also Cherita Chen (fifteen).

SAMANTHA

Hi, Cherita.

CHERITA

Chut up.

15

Also there are Donnie's two best friends, Sean Smith (sixteen) and Ronald Fisher (fifteen).

RONALD
(raising his hands in victory)
DARKO CHEATS DEATH! Man . . . you're famous! I called you, like a jillion times last night!

DONNIE
We went to a hotel.

RONALD
My dad said he found you on the golf course. Are you sleepwalking again?

DONNIE
I don't wanna talk about it.

SEAN
Now that you're famous, you gotta have a smoke.

Sean hands Donnie a Marlboro Red and he takes it, looking over at Samantha and Joanie.

DONNIE
What happens if you tell Mom and Dad about this, Samantha?

SAMANTHA
You'll put Ariel in the garbage disposal.

JOANIE
So . . . grody.

Sean, Ronald and Donnie light up. Ronald is the most amateur-looking.

SEAN
Hey, Cherita . . . want a cigarette?

CHERITA
Chut up.

RONALD
(mimicking)
Chut up!

Go back to China, bitch!

DONNIE

Leave her alone, man.

Cherita looks over at Donnie . . . her quiet devastation poorly hidden.

EXT./INT. MIDDLESEX RIDGE SCHOOL – MORNING (8 AM)

The following montage is three long steadicam shots in the main school hallway and courtyard.

We follow Donnie and his friends as they pour out of the back of the emergency exit of the school bus to 'Head Over Heels' by Tears for Fears.

We pick up teachers Karen Pomeroy (twenty-seven), Dr Kenneth Monnitoff (thirty) and Kitty Farmer (forty-two), with Jim Cunningham, as they make their way through the hallways.

Swarms of girls surround Donnie, as he makes his way to his locker. There is a huge smile on his face.

We reveal Gretchen Ross (fifteen) . . . we see Principal Cole (thirty-eight) and then Samantha's dance team (Sparkle Motion) practising their routine in the courtyard.

We follow Ms Pomeroy into English class . . . then time-lapse dissolve through the doorway . . .

INT. ENGLISH CLASS – DAY (8:30 AM)

Ms Pomeroy has been reading from The Destructors *by Graham Greene.*

MS POMEROY

'There would be headlines in the papers. Even the grown-up gangs who ran the betting at the all-in wrestling and the barrow-boys would hear with respect how Old Misery's house had been destroyed. It was as though this plan had been with him all his life, pondered through the seasons, now in his fifteenth year crystallised with the pain of puberty.'

17

Donnie sits in the front.

What is Graham Greene trying to communicate in this passage? Why do the children break into Old Misery's house?

Joanie James raises her hand.

Joanie.

JOANIE
They wanted to rob him.

MS POMEROY
Joanie, if you had actually read the short story . . . which, at a whopping thirteen pages must have kept you up all night, you would know that the children find a great deal of money hidden in a mattress. But they burn it.

The class gives an 'Awww.' Joanie blushes.

Donnie Darko, perhaps, given your recent brush with mass destruction, you can give us your opinion?

DONNIE
Well . . . they say it right when they are ripping the place to shreds. When they flood the house. That like . . . destruction is a form of creation. So the fact that they burn the money is . . . ironic. They just want to see what happens when they tear the world apart. (*Beat.*) They want to change things.

Gretchen Ross stands at the doorway to the classroom.

MS POMEROY
May we help you?

GRETCHEN
I just registered, and I think they put me in the wrong English class.

Ms Pomeroy studies her.

MS POMEROY
You look like you belong here.

GRETCHEN
Umm, where do I sit?

Ms Pomeroy thinks for a moment. There are several empty seats.

> MS POMEROY
> Sit next to the boy you think is the cutest. Girls get up.

The whole class begins to freak out. The girls all get out of their seats . . . eating this up. Ronald fixes his hair.

> Quiet! Let her choose.

Without hesitation, Gretchen scans the class for every guy. As she gracefully takes her seat next to Donnie, they make eye contact. Donnie grins ear to ear.

The class freaks out laughing.

INT. TAURUS – SUNSET (MONDAY NIGHT, 6 PM)

Eddie drives Donnie down Old Gun Road, a windy back-road that goes towards the country.

> EDDIE
> So how was school today?

> DONNIE
> It was great. We had peanut-butter sandwiches and apples and honey at snacktime. And then during show-and-tell my stuffed walrus was a big hit.

> EDDIE
> Good Lord. (*Beat.*) So the construction guys say it'll take about a week to fix the roof. Damn airline better not fuck us on the shingle match.

> DONNIE
> Do they know yet?

> EDDIE
> Know what?

> DONNIE
> Where it came from.

> EDDIE
> No . . . apparently they can't tell us what happened yet. Something about a matching serial number that got burned.

(*Beat.*) I had to sign a form saying I wouldn't talk to anyone about it.

                    DONNIE
So we're not supposed to tell anybody what nobody knows?

                    EDDIE
You tell Dr Thurman whatever you want.

Suddenly, Eddie slams on the brakes and the station wagon comes to a sudden stop.

Oh, shit!

                    DONNIE
Grandma Death.

Standing in the road directly in front of the car is Roberta Sparrow (101 years old, aka Grandma Death).

Grandma Death lives in a modest brick house that sits back in a huge grassy field that overlooks the entire town. Her mailbox sits on the edge of Old Gun Road.

EXT. OLD GUN ROAD – NEXT

Donnie gets out of the car and takes Grandma Death's hand, walking her back towards her mailbox. He opens it for her.

                    DONNIE
No mail today. (*Smiles.*) Maybe tomorrow.

Grandma Death smiles back at him . . . and begins to walk slowly back to her house. She then turns and takes Donnie's hands into her frail grip.

                    GRANDMA DEATH
                    (*speaking slowly*)
Every living creature . . . on this earth . . . (*Beat.*) . . . dies alone.

Donnie stands there silently for a moment, and then Grandma Death turns back towards her house.

EXT. DR THURMAN'S RANCH – SUNSET

We see a large colonial rancher in the distance.

Dr Lilian Thurman (fifty-eight) is a beautiful older woman.

> DR THURMAN
> Your mother said that you've been skipping cycles of your
> medication.

> DONNIE
> I've been taking it. I just like to make her feel guilty for all
> of this. You know, abuse her. Psychologically.

> DR THURMAN
> All of this . . . certainly isn't your mother's fault, Donald.

He is quiet for a moment.

> DONNIE
> So, I met a new friend.

> DR THURMAN
> Would you like to talk about this friend?

> DONNIE
> His name is Frank.

> DR THURMAN
> Frank.

> DONNIE
> I think he saved my life.

> DR THURMAN
> How so?

> DONNIE
> Don't you watch the news?

> DR THURMAN
> I don't own a television.

> DONNIE
> A jet engine fell on my house . . . landed on my bed. While I was
> talking to Frank on the golf course.

*Dr Thurman looks at him for a long beat, analysing whether or not
he is telling her the truth.*

> I'm not kidding.

Concerned, Dr Thurman leans in closer.

> DR THURMAN
> Frank . . . instructed you . . . to get out of bed . . . just before this happened.

> DONNIE
> He said to follow him.

> DR THURMAN
> Follow him where?

> DONNIE
> Into the future. (*Beat.*) Then he said that the world was coming to an end.

He rubs his arm, where the numbers are still drawn lightly.

> DR THURMAN
> Do you believe that the world is coming to an end?

> DONNIE
> (*long beat*)
> No. (*Beat.*) That' s stupid.

INT. MIDDLESEX RIDGE SCHOOL – HALLWAY

In the empty school hallway . . . a gigantic tidal wave forms in the distance and comes crashing towards us between the lockers.

INT. FAMILY ROOM – NIGHT (EARLY TUESDAY MORNING, 2 AM)

Donnie lies on the couch . . . fast asleep. His eyes slowly open.

There . . . standing in the corner of the room in the shadows is Frank.

> FRANK
> Wake up, Donnie.

INT. MIDDLESEX RIDGE SCHOOL – NIGHT

In the dark school hallway, Donnie rounds the corner with a flashlight, a can of spray paint and an axe. Frank stands in the same hallway where the tidal wave crashed.

INT. SCHOOL BASEMENT – NEXT

Donnie shines the flashlight through the basement. He approaches some old piping.

Donnie puts the axe back over his shoulder and then lowers it fiercely. The smashing of metal against metal echoes through the huge room.

Title card:

OCTOBER 4 1988

EXT. BUS STOP – MORNING (7 AM)

The same group stands and waits for the bus. The guys smoke. Cherita stands alone. Samantha is reading something to Joanie.

> SAMANTHA
> *(reading)*
> And the prince was led into a world of strange and beautiful magic.

> JOANIE
> Wow.

Donnie grabs the piece of paper from his sister.

> DONNIE
> *(reading out loud)*
> *The Last Unicorn!* By Samantha Darko!

> SAMANTHA
> Donnie! Give it back!

He pushes her away.

> You're wrinkling it!

> SEAN
> Hey, it's 7:45. The bus shoulda been here like twenty minutes ago.

> RONALD
> Maybe Martha Moo finally went nuts and hijacked the bus.

SEAN
(*excited*)
You know, there's like this rule. We get to go home at 7:55.

RONALD
There's no rule!

SEAN
Fuck yeah there is! If the bus doesn't show up in thirty minutes, you're *supposed* to go *straight* home.

DONNIE
Yeah . . . he's right. Because if we keep waiting some guy in a van might pull up and try to molest us. And then our parents could sue the school board.

Everyone starts to get excited . . . looking down the road to see if the bus is coming.

Sean's watch hits 7:55. No bus.

SEAN
All right! 7:55. Everybody goes home.

RONALD
Let's go to Donnie's house. His parents are both at work.

The three guys begin walking.

DONNIE
Come on, Sam, you can call Joanie's mom from home.

The two girls follow them. Cherita stands at the corner.

Hey, Cherita . . . you should go home.

SEAN
Yeah, if you're still here and the bus comes we'll get in trouble.

CHERITA
Chut up.

SEAN
Hey, porky pig, I hope you get molested!

Suddenly, Emily Bates (ten) and Susie Bates (eight) run up to the bus stop.

                              EMILY
Hey! Our mom said that school is cancelled today because it's
flooded!

                              JOANIE
No . . . way.

A horrible expression appears on Donnie's face.

INT. MIDDLESEX RIDGE SCHOOL – MORNING

*A janitor named Leroy (fifty-five) stands at the end of the hall with
Principal Cole. Water rushes past their feet down the steps.*

                              LEROY
I got twelve classrooms full of water. All coming from a busted
water main.

                          PRINCIPAL COLE
What else?

                              LEROY
What else? Shit, Principal Cole, you ain't gonna believe what
else.

EXT. BACK COURTYARD – MORNING

*They stand before the bronze Middlesex mongrel. Spray-painted on
the concrete before it is the phrase:* THEY MADE ME DO IT.

*There are papers strewn everywhere. Embedded in the head of the
mongrel is an axe.*

                          PRINCIPAL COLE
Christ. Is that an axe?

                              LEROY
Yep.

                          PRINCIPAL COLE
How did this happen?

                              LEROY
                             (*Beat.*)
I guess they made him do it.

Leroy can't help himself. He begins to laugh.

PRINCIPAL COLE

You're fired.

Principal Cole walks off.

EXT. BUS STOP 2 – EARLY MORNING (8:15 AM)

Donnie, Sean, Ronald, Samantha and Joanie, Emily and Susie walk from their bus stop.

RONALD

School's closed! Everybody go home!

EMILY

Nuh-uh.

SAMANTHA

Yeah-huh. A cat burglar broke in and trashed everything.

Susie talks with Emily. Joanie and Samantha listen in.

EMILY

Mom said that the boys' locker room looked like a swimming pool . . . and that they found faeces everywhere.

SUSIE

What are faeces?

EMILY

Baby mice.

SUSIE

Awww.

JOANIE

Oh my God, that is so grody.

EXT. BUS STOP 3 – NEXT

Sean looks down to another bus stop down the street.

SEAN

School's cancelled!

A bunch of young kids scream out . . . jumping up and down.

26

Donnie approaches another corner alone. Ricky Danforth (seventeen) and Seth Devlin (eighteen) stand with Gretchen.

> SETH
> *(smoking a cigarette)*
> Has anyone ever told you that you're sexy?

> RICKY

I like your boobs.

Gretchen looks at them with disgust.

Donnie walks into the group.

> DONNIE

Hey . . .

> GRETCHEN

Hey . . .

> DONNIE

School's cancelled.

They look at one another . . . surprised.

> GRETCHEN
> *(to Donnie)*

Wanna walk me home?

> DONNIE

Sure.

They quickly begin to walk off. Seth and Ricky look off at them, furious.

> GRETCHEN

Don't look so freaked.

> DONNIE

I'm not. But you should check your backpack 'cause those guys love to steal shit.

> GRETCHEN

Fuck them.

Gretchen smiles at Donnie, and then turns back and gives them the middle finger.

Donnie and Gretchen walk along the sidewalk together.

DONNIE

So . . . you just moved here?

GRETCHEN

Yeah. My parents got divorced. My mom has a restraining order against my stepdad. (*Beat.*) He has . . . emotional problems.

DONNIE

Oh. I . . . have those too. (*Beat.*) What kind of problems does your dad have?

GRETCHEN

(*long beat*)

He stabbed my mom four times in the chest.

Donnie is shocked.

DONNIE

Wow. Did he go to jail?

GRETCHEN

He fled. They still can't find him. (*Beat.*) My mom and I had to change our names and stuff. I thought Gretchen sounded kind of cool.

DONNIE

I'm sorry. I was in jail once. (*Beat.*) I accidentally burned down this house. It was abandoned. I got held back in school again. Can't drive until I'm eighteen. (*babbling*) I think when I grow up I want to be a painter. Or maybe a writer or maybe both. Then I'll write a book and then draw the illustrations like a comic book. You know, change things.

GRETCHEN

Donnie Darko is a cool name. Sounds like a superhero.

DONNIE

What makes you think I'm not?

Gretchen smiles.

Gretchen looks over at her house.

> GRETCHEN
> I should go. For physics, Monnitoff says I have to write an
> essay on the greatest invention ever to benefit mankind.

> DONNIE
> That's easy. Antiseptics.

She gives him a look.

> I mean, the whole sanitation thing. Joseph Lister . . . 1895.
> Before antiseptics there was no sanitation, especially in
> medicine.

> GRETCHEN
> You mean soap?

> DONNIE
> Don't knock soap. Without it, disease would spread rapidly. If
> we ran out . . . you and I would never live to see the year 2000.

> GRETCHEN
> Wonder where we'll be then.

> DONNIE
> The best thing about soap is that it's the only thing on earth
> than can never get dirty. No matter what crap you throw on
> it . . . it always rubs off. And there it is again . . . perfect.

> GRETCHEN
> Until it withers away.

She stares at him for a moment.

> DONNIE
> It's a good thing the school was flooded today.

> GRETCHEN
> Why is that?

> DONNIE
> We never would have had this conversation.

She smiles.

You're weird.

                    DONNIE

I'm sorry.

                    GRETCHEN

That was a compliment.

                    DONNIE

Will you go with me?

                    GRETCHEN

Where are we going?

                    DONNIE

No . . . I mean, will you *go* with me? That's like . . . what they call it here. Going together.

                    GRETCHEN
                    (*beat*)

Sure.

She gets up and begins to walk up the hill.

                    DONNIE

Where are you going?

                    GRETCHEN

I'm going home.

Title card:

OCTOBER 6 1988

INT. THERAPIST'S OFFICE – EVENING (THURSDAY, 6 PM)

Dr Thurman sits next to Donnie. His eyes are closed.

                    DR THURMAN

And when I clap my hands twice, you will wake up. Do you understand?

                    DONNIE

Yes.

                    DR THURMAN

So tell me about your day, Donald.

DONNIE

I met a girl.

DR THURMAN

What is her name?

DONNIE

Gretchen. We're going together now.

DR THURMAN

Do you think a lot about girls?

DONNIE

Yes.

DR THURMAN

How are things going at school?

DONNIE

I think about girls a lot.

DR THURMAN

I asked you about school.

DONNIE

I think about . . . fucking a lot during school.

DR THURMAN

What else do you think about during school?

DONNIE

I think . . . about . . . *who's the boss.*

DR THURMAN

Who is the boss?

DONNIE

I just turn down the volume and think about fucking Alyssa
Milano.

DR THURMAN

What about your *family*, Donnie?

DONNIE

No, I don't think about fucking my family. That's sick.

DR THURMAN

Donnie . . . I want to hear about your friend Frank.

31

Donnie is now undoing his belt. He is no longer paying attention.

Dr Thurman quickly claps her hands. Donnie jolts awake . . .
disoriented.

INT. ENGLISH CLASS – DAY (FRIDAY, 8:30 AM)

Donnie sits with his eyes wide open, staring at something.

> POLICE OFFICER
> (*out of shot*)
>
> Aaron Armitige . . . Cherita Chen.

Donnie's face has gone white.

> PRINCIPAL COLE
>
> Donald Darko.

We reveal on the blackboard the phrase 'They made me do it',
written over and over again.

We reveal two Police Officers standing next to Principal Cole in the
corner of the classroom.

Donnie gets up and walks over to the board and writes the phrase.

He then sits down again without hesitation.

The Police Officer hesitates for a moment, lingering over Donnie's
penmanship. He then places a '?' next to Donnie's name on the
roster. Ms Pomeroy makes eye-contact with him.

INT. HEALTH CLASS – AFTERNOON (FRIDAY, 1 PM)

We pull back from a television: a cloud formation blows across the
screen revealing a logo that reads CUNNING VISION PRODUCTIONS.
A series of interviews follows . . . infomercial-style.

> LINDA CONNIE
>
> And what I realised was that for my entire life I was a victim of
> my own *fear*. I was *feeding fear with food* . . . and finally . . .
> I looked in the mirror. Not just *in the mirror*. I looked *through*
> the mirror. And in that image I saw my *ego reflection*.

Donnie's health class is assembled in uniform rows in front of a
television cart. Ms Farmer paces in front of them.

SHANDA RIESMAN
(*with her arm around her geeky son*)
. . . and for two years I thought it was *normal* for a fifteen-
year-old to wet the bed.

Laughter from the students.

MS FARMER
QUIET!

SHANDA RIESMAN
(*choking up*)
We tried everything. But the solution was there . . . all along.

LARRY RIESMAN
(*bursts out emotionally*)
I'm not *afraid* any more!

A montage of 'family' imagery follows.

NARRATOR
All across America . . . people have come together to join
hands. People who believe that human life is too important . . .
too valuable to be controlled by FEAR.

*A middle-aged man walks out onto a country patio. It is Jim
Cunningham . . . the guy from the golf course.*

JIM CUNNINGHAM
Hello. My name is Jim Cunningham. And welcome to
'Controlling Fear'.

The title CONTROLLING FEAR *appears on the screen . . . followed by*
PART ONE: ATTITUDINAL BELIEFS.

FRANK
(*voice-over.*)
Pay close attention, you could miss something.

Donnie stares at the screen . . . at Jim Cunningham.

EXT. OLD GUN RUINS – AFTERNOON (FRIDAY MAGIC HOUR, 4:30 PM)

*The ruins of a brick chimney sit in the middle of a field. Donnie,
Sean and Ronald have lined up several empty beer bottles, cans and
stuffed animals on the hearth.*

They take turns blasting these targets with a BB gun.

Blam! A can falls over. Ronald hands the gun to Donnie. Sean pulls out a bottle of Raspberry Night Train and takes a sip. He hands the bottle to Ronald.

> RONALD
>
> What's this shit?

> SEAN
>
> Raspberry.

He takes a big sip . . . which results in a dry heave.

> RONALD
>
> Raspberry. That's good shit.

Donnie aims the crosshairs on Smurfette's head. He pulls the trigger. Smurfette falls over.

> Wicked!

> SEAN
>
> No more fuckin' for her.

> RONALD
>
> Smurfette doesn't fuck.

> SEAN
>
> Bullshit. Smurfette fucks all the other smurfs. That's why Papa Smurf made her, 'cause the other smurfs were getting too horny.

> RONALD
>
> Not *Vanity*. He's homo.

Blam! A bottle shatters.

> SEAN
>
> Then she fucks 'em all while Vanity watches. And Papa Smurf *films* it.

Ronald takes another sip of Night Train . . . followed by another dry heave. Blam! A bottle breaks.

> DONNIE
>
> First of all . . . Papa Smurf didn't create Smurfette. Gargamel did. She was sent in as Gargamel's evil spy with the intention of destroying the smurf village. But the overwhelming Goodness

of the Smurf Way of Life transformed her into the Smurfette we all know and love. And as for the whole gang-bang scenario . . . it just couldn't happen. Smurfs are *asexual*. They probably don't even have reproductive organs down there under those little white pants. The only reason they exist is because of magic spells and witchcraft . . . which is all a bunch of bullshit if you ask me. (*Beat.*) That's what's so illogical about the smurfs . . . what's the point of living if you don't even have a dick?

Donnie aims the gun . . . pulls the trigger. Blam! A bottle breaks.

RONALD

Dammit, Donnie! Why do you always gotta get all smart on us!

Donnie takes the bottle of Night Train and takes a small sip.

Their conversation is interrupted by the squealing of tyres.

EXT. OLD GUN ROAD – NEXT (MAGIC HOUR, 5 PM)

Down the hill a Dodge minivan is stopped on Old Gun Road. Grandma Death is once again in the middle of the street.

DONNIE

Grandma Death.

Ms Farmer leans her head out of the window.

MS FARMER

Excuse me!

Grandma Death doesn't hear her. She wanders around in circles. Furious, Ms Farmer gets out of the car and walks over to the old woman, walking her by the shoulders back to her driveway.

Please stay out of the road, Ms Sparrow. If this happens again I'm going to call social services.

Ms Farmer gets back behind the wheel and they drive off.

Grandma Death lurks around her mailbox.

RONALD

How old is Grandma Death?

DONNIE

A hundred and one, I think. Every day she does the same thing. But there's never any mail.

35

Grandma Death approaches the mailbox.

> SEAN
>
> Here we go . . . this could be it.

She opens it . . . then closes it. Walks away.

> RONALD
>
> Awww. That sucks.

She approaches the box again . . .

> SEAN
>
> Wait a minute . . . we may *still* have mail . . .

Opens it . . . closes it. Walks away.

> RONALD
>
> Noooo!

They continue to watch her, sipping liquor into the sunset, as Grandma Death repeats this act like an ancient wind-up doll.

INT. FAMILY ROOM − EVENING (FRIDAY, 7 PM)

Donnie lies on the couch watching television . . . where there is a news story about the flooded school. Several construction workers are packing up their things.

INT. UPSTAIRS BATHROOM − MOMENTS LATER (7:15 PM)

Looking nauseous, Donnie opens the medicine cabinet and retrieves his pills. He takes four of them. Donnie takes a drink of water, closing his eyes. He puts the pills back and closes the cabinet.

In the mirror's reflection is Frank. Donnie jumps.

> FRANK
>
> You got away with it. Don't worry.

Donnie reaches his hand out towards Frank and it presses against an invisible wall, as if he were pressing his hand against liquid glass.

> DONNIE
>
> How can you do that?

FRANK

I can do anything I want . . . and so can you . . .

Donnie stares closely at Frank. He then removes his hands and moves back away from him.

EXT. MIDDLESEX SCHOOL AUDITORIUM – EVENING (7:15 PM)

A sign reads: EMERGENCY PTA MEETING TONIGHT.

INT. AUDITORIUM – EVENING (7:15 PM)

Parents and teachers convene in front of the auditorium entrance. Kitty Farmer hands out xeroxed pages of something.

Eddie and Rose chit-chat with other concerned parents.

Ms Pomeroy approaches Kitty Farmer.

MS POMEROY

What are you trying to accomplish here?

MS FARMER
(*indignant*)

There was urine and faeces flooded in my office.

INT. AUDITORIUM – LATER ON

The crowd settles . . . Principal Cole takes the stage.

PRINCIPAL COLE

In co-operation with the county police we have begun an active investigation into the cause of the flooding . . . and our suspects include several of our own students.

Kitty Farmer stands up in her seat near the front row.

MS FARMER

I want to know why this *filth* is being taught to our children.

The crowd stirs.

PRINCIPAL COLE

Kitty, I would appreciate . . . if you would wait . . .

37

Mr Cole . . . not only am I a *teacher* . . . but I am also a *parent* of a Middlesex child. Therefore I am the *only* person here who transcends the parent-teacher bridge.

PRINCIPAL COLE

Kitty . . .

MS FARMER

The bottom line . . . Mr Cole . . . is that there is material being taught to our children that is cause for this destructive behaviour.

She stands up.

I have in my hand Graham Greene's *The Destructors*. This short story is part of my daughter's English assignment. In this story several children destroy an elderly man's house from inside out. They destroy his house without motive, without moral consequence. They destroy private property . . . and they get away with it.

Ms Pomeroy shakes her head bitterly.

And how do they do this? They *flood* the house . . . by breaking through the water main!

PRINCIPAL COLE
(*trying to calm her*)
This meeting of the PTA was called to inform the parents of our ongoing investigation . . .

MS FARMER
(*enraged*)
I AM THE PTA! And I say that this *filth* is directly related to this vandalism.

Applause from the crowd.

I think this garbage should be removed.

Several shouts of a approval come from the crowd.

INT. UPSTAIRS BATHROOM – EVENING

Donnie continues to converse with Frank.

DONNIE

Why did you make me flood the school?

FRANK

We just want to guide you in the right direction.

DONNIE

Who is . . . we?

FRANK

You'll know soon enough.

DONNIE
(*desperate*)

Where did you come from?

FRANK
(*beat*)

Do you believe in time travel, Donnie?

A moment of silence.

SAMANTHA

Who are you talking to?

Donnie turns to see Samantha standing in the doorway. Frank is gone.

INT. AUDITORIUM — NIGHT

*A heated debate among the parents is under way. Frustrated, Rose
stands up. Karen Pomeroy is furious.*

ROSE

Excuse me . . . but what is the real issue here? The PTA doesn't
ban books from school.

MS FARMER

The PTA is here to acknowledge that there is pornography in
our school's curriculum.

MS POMEROY
(*standing up*)

My *God* . . . woman, are you drunk?

MS FARMER

Excuse me? You need to go back to grad school.

                              ROSE
                           (to Kitty)
              Do you even know who Graham Greene is?

                            MS FARMER
                           (to Rose)
                 I think we've all seen *Bonanza*.

*Ms Pomeroy is disgusted. Rose and Eddie burst out laughing, grab
their coats and leave.*

EXT. WIZARD'S ARCADE – AFTERNOON (SATURDAY, 1 PM)

*Donnie and Gretchen play a Sega race-car driving game. Donnie
drives a souped-up red Ferarri through the Grand Canyon.*

                            GRETCHEN
        So when you sleepwalk can you remember afterward? Like, do
        you dream?

                             DONNIE
        No. I just wake up and I look around, try to figure out where
        I am . . . how I got there.

                            GRETCHEN
        My dad said never wake a sleepwalker . . . because they could
        drop dead.

The Trans-Am crashes head on into a tree. Game Over.

                             DONNIE
        It's like this force . . . that's in your brain. But sometimes it
        grows bigger . . . and it spreads down into your arms and
        legs . . . and it just sends you someplace.

                            GRETCHEN
        So when you sleepwalk you go somewhere familiar?

                             DONNIE
        No. Every time I wake up somewhere different. Sometimes my
        bike is laying there next to me. Like once when I woke up on
        the edge of this cliff up on Carpathian Ridge.

                            GRETCHEN
        And you'd never been there before?

They sit silently for a moment.

Donnie?

> DONNIE

Yeah?

> GRETCHEN

Do you ever feel as though there's always someone watching you?

> DONNIE

Why?

> GRETCHEN

Well . . . maybe someone is like . . . giving you these dream steroids. And sleepwalking . . . is someone showing you the way.

Title card:

OCTOBER 13 1988

INT. ENGLISH CLASS – MORNING (THURSDAY, 8 AM)

Donnie stands in front of the class. Ms Pomeroy sits behind her desk. On the chalkboard is: 'Poetry Day'.

> DONNIE

'A storm is coming, Frank says. A storm that will swallow the children . . . and I will deliver them from the kingdom of pain. (*Beat.*) I will deliver the children to their doorsteps. I will send the monsters back to the underground. I will send them back to a place where no one can see them . . . except for me. Because I am Donnie Darko.'

Donnie returns to his seat. Ms Pomeroy stares at him intensely.

> MS POMEROY

Who is Frank?

> DONNIE

A six-foot-tall bunny rabbit.

The class begins to laugh. Donnie looks over at Gretchen.

Ms Farmer stands next to the television where Jim Cunningham narrates the Lifeline tutorial.

JIM CUNNINGHAM
And so, now, let us begin Lifeline Exercise No 1.

PLEASE PRESS STOP NOW *appears on the screen.*

Ms Farmer stops the tape and moves to the blackboard. On it she has drawn a horizontal line book-ended by the words 'Love' and 'Fear'.

MS FARMER
As you can see, the Lifeline is controlled by two polar extremes: 'Fear' and 'Love'. Fear is in the negative energy spectrum. Love is in the positive energy spectrum.

SEAN
(*to Donnie*)
No duh.

MS FARMER
Excuse me? (*defensive*) 'No duh' is a product of fear.

She stares them down for a moment . . . shaking her head.

(*handing out cards*) Now on each card is a *Character Dilemma* which applies to the Lifeline. Please read each character dilemma aloud . . . and place an X on the Lifeline in the appropriate place.

The students read their cards.

We'll start in the front.

Cherita Chen stands up and walks over to the blackboard. Ms Farmer pulls up large white cards that have black-and-white animated cartoons on them.

CHERITA
Juanita has an important math test today. She has known about the test for several weeks, but has not studied. In order to keep from failing her class, Juanita decides that she will cheat on the math test.

Cherita places an X near the 'Fear' end of the lifeline.

MS FARMER

Good. Next.

Donnie watches as several more students interpret their respective human dilemmas.

Finally . . . it is his turn.

DONNIE

Ling Ling finds a wallet on the ground filled with money. She takes the wallet to the address on the driver's licence but keeps the money inside the wallet.

Donnie looks at the blackboard.

I'm sorry, Ms Farmer, I just don't get this.

MS FARMER
(*impatient*)

Just place an X in the appropriate place on the Lifeline.

DONNIE

I just don't get this. Everything can't be lumped into two categories. That's too simple.

MS FARMER

The Lifeline is divided that way.

DONNIE

Well, life isn't that simple. So what if Ling Ling kept the cash and returned the wallet. That has nothing to do with either fear or love.

MS FARMER
(*impatient*)

Fear and love are the deepest of human emotions.

DONNIE

Well, yeah . . . OK, but you're not listening to me. There are other things that need to be taken into account here. Like the whole spectrum of human emotion. You're just lumping everything into these two categories . . . and like denying everything else.

43

Ms Farmer stares at Donnie vehemently. She can't believe what she's hearing.

People aren't that simple.

> MS FARMER
> (*not knowing how to argue with him*)
> If you don't complete the assignment you'll get a zero for the day.

Donnie thinks for a moment . . . and then raises his hand.

INT. PRINCIPAL COLE'S OFFICE – AFTERNOON (2 PM)

Donnie and his parents sit in front of Principal Cole.

> PRINCIPAL COLE
> Donald . . . let me preface this by saying that your Iowa test scores are . . . (*looking down at the file*) . . . intimidating. (*rubbing his temples*) So . . . let's go over this again. What exactly did you say to Ms Farmer?

Donnie does not answer. We reveal Ms Farmer standing in the corner.

> MS FARMER
> (*furious*)
> He asked me to . . . forcibly insert the Lifeline exercise card into my anus.

Silence. Rose looks down, furious. Eddie lets out a snort laugh which he tries to conceal with a cough. It doesn't work.

INT. TEACHERS' LOUNGE/OFFICE – MOMENTS LATER (2:15 PM)

Eddie and Donnie exit Cole's office, moving on while Rose approaches Kitty, who looks visibly shaken.

> ROSE
> Kitty, I don't know what to say. They've suspended him for two days. (*Beat.*) Ever since this jet engine fiasco, I honestly don't know what has gotten into him.

> MS FARMER
> Rose, I'll tell you this because our daughters have been on dance team together for two years and I respect you as a *woman*. But

after witnessing your son's behaviour today I have . . . significant doubts . . . (*stopping herself*) Our paths through life must be righteous. I urge you to go home and look in the mirror and pray that your son does not succumb to the path of fear.

Kitty Farmer turns and walks away.

EXT. DARKO BACKYARD/PATIO – SUNSET (MAGIC HOUR, 5:30 PM)

Samantha jumps up and down on the trampoline.

INT. DONNIE'S ROOM – NIGHT (5:30 PM)

Donnie walks into his room again for the first time since the accident, looking around at the new furniture, paint and carpet. Everything is perfect.

Elizabeth appears in the doorway behind him with a cordless phone in her hand.

> ELIZABETH
> (*into the phone*)
> Oh my God, remember that gym teacher, Ms Farmer? (*Beat.*) Yeah. Well I guess my brother called her a fat bitch today in class and got suspended. And my parents just bought him all of this new shit. (*Beat.*) Yeah, I know. I wish a jet engine would have fallen on my room.

INT. MARINO'S ITALIAN BISTRO – NIGHT (6 PM)

Eddie and Rose sit across from one another at the bistro patio . . . having a quiet dinner to themselves.

> ROSE
> He's too old to be behaving this way.

Eddie considers this.

> EDDIE
> Oh, I say we buy him a moped.

INT. DONNIE'S ROOM – NIGHT (7 PM)

Donnie lies in bed . . . looking up at the ceiling. He then rolls over and looks at the calendar on his wall. The days of the month of

October are marked off with an X in each square. Tacked onto the calendar is a drawing of Frank.

> DONNIE
> 28 days, 6 hours, 42 minutes, 12 seconds.

INT. PHYSICS CLASS – DAY (FRIDAY, 2:30 PM)

As everyone is leaving class, Donnie stays behind.

> DONNIE
> Dr Monnitoff?

> DR MONNITOFF
> Donnie.

> DONNIE
> I know that this is gonna sound kinda weird . . . but do you know anything about time travel?

Dr Monnitoff pauses, turns and looks at Donnie. He seems to know something.

INT. PHYSICS CLASS – LATER ON

Dr Monnitoff has drawn a diagram on the blackboard. In his hand he holds a copy of Stephen Hawking's A Brief History of Time.

> DR MONNITOFF
> So . . . according to Hawking . . . wormholes might be able to provide a short cut for jumping between two distant regions of space–time.

> DONNIE
> So . . . in order to travel back in time you'd have to have a big spaceship or something that can travel faster than the speed of light –

> DR MONNITOFF
> Theoretically.

> DONNIE
> – and be able to find one of these wormholes.

DR MONNITOFF

A wormhole with an Einstein–Rosen bridge, which is,
theoretically . . . a wormhole in space controlled by man.

DONNIE

So . . . that's it?

DR MONNITOFF

The basic principals of time travel are there. (*Beat.*) So you
have the vessel and the portal. And the vessel can be anything.
Most likely a spacecraft.

EXT. SCHOOL COURTYARD – NEXT

Cherita Chen listens to this conversation intently.

INT. PHYSICS CLASS – NEXT

DONNIE

Like a DeLorean.

DR MONNITOFF
(*smiling*)

A metal craft of any kind.

*Donnie stares at him intently. Dr Monnitoff walks over to his desk
and picks up a book.*

Don't tell anyone that I gave you this. (*Beat.*) The woman who
wrote it . . . used to teach here a long time ago. She was a nun
for many many years and then overnight she just became this
entirely different person. She up and left the Church, wrote this
book, and started teaching science.

Donnie takes the battered book . . . we see the cover.

INT. SCHOOL MAIN HALLWAY – MOMENTS LATER

*Donnie stands before an array of old photographs. We zoom in to a
black-and-white photograph of a young Roberta Sparrow standing
in a class photograph dated 1944.*

Donnie looks down at the book . . . and then at the photograph.

DONNIE

Roberta Sparrow . . . Grandma Death.

INT. KITCHEN – NIGHT (FRIDAY, 6 PM)

Donnie sits down for dinner with his family.

DONNIE

It's called *The Philosophy of Time Travel*.

ELIZABETH

What does time travel have to do with philosophy?

DONNIE

Guess who wrote it?

No one seems to know.

Grandma Death.

ROSE

That is a terrible nickname.

EDDIE

Grandma Death.

DONNIE
(*to Eddie*)

You know, Roberta Sparrow. We almost hit her with the car
the other day.

ROSE

I've heard she's loaded.

The family is taken aback.

EDDIE

You're right. Roberta Sparrow was famous for her gem
collections. Kids used to try and steal stuff from her all the
time. Over the years . . . as she got older she became more and
more of a recluse . . . now she just likes to stay up there all by
herself.

DONNIE

I guess she just lost faith in the world.

EXT. DARKO BACKYARD – SUNSET (SATURDAY, 5:30 PM)

Slow motion: Donnie and Gretchen jump up and down on the trampoline, lost among falling autumn leaves.

INT. THERAPIST'S OFFICE – DAY (SUNDAY, 12 PM)

Donnie is back on Dr Thurman's couch.

> DR THURMAN
>
> How many times have you seen Frank?

> DONNIE
>
> Four times . . . so far.

> DR THURMAN
>
> Can anyone else see him?

> DONNIE
>
> I don't think so. It's like a TV station. And they're tuned into mine and no one else's.

> DR THURMAN
>
> Who is they? Is Frank a part of some larger group?

> DONNIE
>
> I don't know. Gretchen has a theory. That Frank is a sign. I told her I thought it was ridiculous.

> DR THURMAN
>
> A sign from whom?

> DONNIE
> *(changing the subject)*
>
> I think that Frank wants me to go talk to this woman. *(holding up the book)* She wrote a book about time travel. Frank asked me if I believed in time travel. That can't just be a random coincidence. *(Beat.)* My dad almost hit her with the car the other day, and she said the creepiest thing. She said that every living creature on this earth dies alone.

> DR THURMAN
>
> How does that make you feel?

DONNIE

It reminded my of my dog Callie.

DR THURMAN

Is Callie still around?

DONNIE

No. She died when I was eight. We couldn't find her for days.
She went and crawled underneath our back porch . . .

DR THURMAN

Do you feel alone right now?

He looks at her for a moment.

DONNIE

I'd like to believe that I'm not . . . but I've just never seen any
proof. So I just choose not to bother with it. It's like I could
spend my whole life thinking about it . . . debating it in my
head. Weighing the pros and cons. And in the end I still
wouldn't have any proof. So . . . I don't even debate it any
more. Because it's absurd. (*Beat.*) I don't want to be alone.
(*Beat.*) So does that make me like an atheist?

DR THURMAN

No. That makes you keep searching.

Donnie takes this in for a moment.

INT. FAMILY ROOM – EVENING (SUNDAY, 7:15 PM)

*Eddie and Dr Fisher watch the Redskins game. Ronald and Donnie
watch the game in the family room.*

EDDIE

Ahhh . . . We need Theisman.

DR FISHER

We need a miracle.

INT. KITCHEN – NEXT

*Rose and Anne Fisher (forty-five) share a bottle of wine at the
kitchen table.*

ANNE

And so his tapes made me realise that for forty-six years I have been a prisoner of fear. Rose, you have to meet Jim Cunningham. (*taking a sip of wine*) I can't believe he's not married.

Samantha bounces through the kitchen into the family room wearing a Dorothy outfit from The Wizard of Oz.

INT. FAMILY ROOM – NEXT

Donnie sits back in the La-Z-Boy, dozing off . . .

John Madden's CBS chalkboard unfolds on the TV screen. Madden traces his electronic lines across the screen, tracing the movement of the players . . . as their images are frozen in time.

Donnie's eyes close . . . and then re-open.

Donnie turns his head and sees that the room is momentarily bathed in artificial white light as if God hit the slow-motion button during a flash of lightning.

Donnie turns his head and sees that protruding from his father's stomach . . . is a thick spear made of silvery plastic gel.

As Eddie gets up from the couch to walk over to the refrigerator . . . his spear precedes him . . . morphing into an extruded arrow that reaches the refrigerator several seconds before him.

The spear traces the exact geography of his movement through time . . . using his centre of gravity as its axis point.

Donnie turns and sees Samantha skipping from the kitchen . . . as her spear bounces several feet in front of her like a caterpillar. Her spear . . . smaller than her father's . . . is proportional to her mass.

SAMANTHA
(*her voice echoing through the silence*)
Follow the yellow brick road . . .

Donnie looks down at his stomach and sees his own spear protruding outward. It then begins to extrude forward towards the foyer.

He does not follow it. It then retreats back in and beckons him to follow.

Like a child transfixed by a firefly . . . Donnie follows the path of his spear into the foyer.

INT. FOYER/UPSTAIRS HALLWAY – NEXT

Donnie and his spear round the corner and arrive in his parents' bedroom.

INT. MASTER BEDROOM – NIGHT

His spear leads him to the closet. He opens the closet door . . . and the spear leads him down to a box hidden beneath his father's shoe rack.

Donnie removes the box from the closet and unlatches it. Inside is a gun. Donnie removes the pistol from the box . . . staring at it with the same childlike expression.

Suddenly . . . Donnie's universe snaps back to normal. The white light strobes . . . the spear has vanished.

Donnie still holds the gun. His expression changes to nervous shock.

His eyes linger over the gun for a moment, he then quickly puts it back in the box . . . and carefully places the box back under the shoe rack.

Title card:

OCTOBER 18 1988

EXT. BUS STOP – MORNING (TUESDAY, 7:30 AM)

The usual bus-stop crew is there. Donnie arrives last . . . by himself. He looks tired and preoccupied.

A plane flies overhead . . . they all look up at the sky.

INT. ENGLISH CLASS – MORNING (8:30 AM)

We see the students placing the Graham Greene books on Ms Pomeroy's desk.

MS POMEROY
It gives me no pleasure to deny you the right to read one of the great writers of the twentieth century. But . . . alas, I have not

yet been elected Queen of the Universe. And until that day I will be forced to obey the rules . . . and so will you. *So . . . if anyone is found carrying this book in school they will be suspended.*

Donnie slips his book into his backpack.

But let's not worry. Someone has already pre-ordered several dozen copies at Sarasota Mall Waldenbooks. Now in Mr Greene's absence we will be reading another classic. Richard Adams' *Watership Down.*

She begins to hand out copies of the paperback novel. Beth Farmer smiles when she sees the cover.

                    BETH
Awww. Bunnies.

                    MS POMEROY
                (whispering in his ear)
Donnie, maybe you and Frank can read this one together.

INT. SCHOOL BATHROOM – MIDDAY (11:30 PM)

Donnie walks along the edge of the school. Suddenly, a figure approaches, grabbing him from behind, placing a switchblade next his throat. It is Seth Devlin.

                    SETH
Did you tell them that I flooded the school?

                    DONNIE
I didn't say shit.

                    SETH
That's not what I heard. Now they think I did it.

                    DONNIE
Well, if you're innocent then you have nothing to worry about.

                    SETH
You know what I think? I think that you did it.

Seth takes the knife and pokes the tip softly into the flesh of Donnie's neck, drawing a small amount of blood.

He pushes Donnie away. Donnie touches his neck in shock.

INT. PHYSICS CLASS – DAY (2:30 PM)

Donnie walks into the classroom and takes his seat next to Gretchen. He is sweating profusely.

Dr Monnitoff is handing out papers. The bell rings. People shuffle out.

> DR MONNITOFF
> Don't forget tomorrow we will be meeting with our partners for the Young Inventors' Fair.

Donnie rubs his finger over his neck wound.

> GRETCHEN
> What happened to your neck?

> DONNIE
> I don't want to talk about it. (*changing the subject*) So what are we going to invent?

EXT. GOLF COURSE FOREST – THAT AFTERNOON (3 PM)

Donnie and Gretchen round the trail.

> GRETCHEN
> Were you ever afraid of the dark?

They pull over to a stop.

> DONNIE
> Why?

She thinks for a moment.

> GRETCHEN
> Babies cry because they're afraid of the dark. And because they have no memories . . . for all they know . . . every night could last for ever. Like, perpetual darkness.

> DONNIE
> Why not just buy your baby a night-light?

> GRETCHEN
> That's not good enough. You've got to go back in time and take all those hours of darkness and pain and replace them . . . with whatever you wanted.

DONNIE

With like, images?

GRETCHEN

Like . . . a Hawaiian sunset . . . the Grand Canyon. Things that remind you how beautiful the world can be.

Donnie stops and takes Gretchen's hand.

DONNIE

You know . . . we've been going together for a week and a half . . .

GRETCHEN

And what?

DONNIE

Well . . .

GRETCHEN

You want to kiss me . . .

Donnie goes in for an awkward kiss . . . but Gretchen turns and denies him.

Donnie turns away . . . embarrassed.

DONNIE

That's alright . . . I understand.

GRETCHEN
(*embarrassed*)
No . . . Donnie, wait. I've never . . .

DONNIE

I always wanted it to be at a time when . . . when it reminds you how beautiful the world can be.

GRETCHEN

Yeah. And right now there's some fat guy over there watching us.

A man in a red jogging suit is standing there in the forest smoking a cigarette. He turns away . . . disappearing into the woods.

EXT. NEIGHBOURHOOD STREET – LATER THAT AFTERNOON (4 PM)

Donnie rides along the sidewalk . . . and skids to a stop, seeing a wallet laying there.

Donnie opens the wallet, looking at the ID. It reads:

> JIM CUNNINGHAM
> 42 POWDERHAM DRIVE
> MIDDLESEX, VA 23113

                    FRANK
          (voice-over, echoing in Donnie's head)
Now you know where he lives.

Donnie looks over and sees that he is in front of Cunningham's Tudor mansion.

INT. KITCHEN – EVENING (7:15 PM)

Donnie sits at the kitchen island with Elizabeth carving a pumpkin.

                    ELIZABETH
So I hear that you have a girlfriend.

                    DONNIE
Yeah.

                    ELIZABETH
What's her name?

                    DONNIE
You're not gonna tell Mom, are you?

                    ELIZABETH
                    (defensive)
Why would I tell Mom?

                    DONNIE
Because you tell Mom everything.

                    ELIZABETH
No I don't. (*Long beat.*) She worries about you.

                    DONNIE
Well, don't worry . . . I'm taking my medication.

ELIZABETH

It's not that. I mean mouthing off to your teachers. I'll admit . . .
when Dad told me what you said to Ms Farmer . . . I laughed
my ass off.

DONNIE

I was just being honest.

ELIZABETH

Yeah . . . well, that's not the way the world works. If you keep
being too honest the world will eventually find a way to
destroy you.

DONNIE

Her name is Gretchen.

ELIZABETH

That's a nice name. (*Beat.*) OK. Let me see it.

*Donnie turns the carved jack-o'-lantern around and we see that it
looks remarkably like Frank.*

INT. THERAPIST'S OFFICE – NIGHT (8 PM)

Rose and Eddie sit in front of Dr Thurman.

ROSE

Thank you for seeing us . . . We . . . just felt that it was time to
discuss . . .

DR THURMAN

What I think is going on with your son.

ROSE

Well, you know about his past. And when you said to look for
signs of aggression . . . He was recently suspended from school
for insulting his gym teacher.

EDDIE

She deserved it.

DR THURMAN

Rose . . . let me just lay out what I believe is happening here.
Donnie's aggressive behaviour seems to stem from his increased
detachment from reality. His inability to cope with the forces in
the world that he perceives to be threatening.

Rose smiles nervously.

Has your son ever told you about Frank?

ROSE

Come again?

DR THURMAN

Frank . . . the giant bunny rabbit?

ROSE

Frank?

DR THURMAN

Donnie is experiencing what is commonly called a daylight hallucination.

ROSE

You're telling me that my son has an imaginary friend?

DR THURMAN

He has described lengthy conversations . . . physical encounters with what I believe to be a manifestation of his subconscious mind.

Rose looks over at Eddie with an expression of panic.

ROSE

I . . . What can we do?

DR THURMAN

I would like to put him through more hypnotherapy . . . and increase his medication.

Eddie looks at Rose . . . who nods in approval.

ROSE

If that's what you think is necessary.

DR THURMAN

But let me remind you that this treatment is . . . experimental.

INT. KITCHEN – NIGHT

Donnie walks into the kitchen and removes a butcher's knife from a drawer.

INT. UPSTAIRS BATHROOM – NIGHT

Donnie stands in front of the bathroom mirror . . . catatonic . . . looking at his reflection.

Frank stands behind him.

Suddenly, Donnie turns around with the butcher's knife and lunges at Frank with all of his weight.

The knife collides with Frank's invisible force field as if it were liquid steel. Donnie lunges repeatedly at Frank with psychotic rage . . . but the knife bounces off.

Title card:

OCTOBER 20 1988

INT. SCHOOL AUDITORIUM – MORNING (10 AM)

The auditorium is packed with Middlesex mongrels. Jim Cunningham takes the stage.

> JIM CUNNINGHAM
> (*shouting*)
> Good morning, mongrels!

> AUDIENCE
> (*scattered voices*)
> Good morning . . .

> JIM CUNNINGHAM
> That's all the gusta you can musta? I said, 'Good morning!'

> AUDIENCE
> (*yelling louder*)
> Good MORNING!

> JIM CUNNINGHAM
> Now that's better . . . but I still sense some students out there . . . who are *afraid* . . . just to say GOOD MORNING!

> AUDIENCE
> (*screaming*)
> GOOD MORNING!

JIM CUNNINGHAM
Are you AFRAID?

AUDIENCE
(*screaming louder*)
GOOD MORNING!

JIM CUNNINGHAM
Now that's what I like to hear. (*suddenly serious*) Because too many young men and women today are paralysed by their fears. They give in to their feelings of self-doubt . . . they surrender their bodies to the temptations of drugs, alcohol and premarital sex. Empty solutions. These are toxic chemicals . . . and disease-spreading behaviour.

A large screen lowers behind him.

I would like to tell you a story today about a young man whose life was destroyed by the instruments of fear. A young man searching for love . . . in all the wrong places. (*shaking his head tragically*) His name was Frank.

On the giant screen an image slide appears of a young cartoon teenager whose eyes are whacked out on drugs. The title appears: HIS NAME WAS FRANK.

Upon hearing the name Frank, Donnie falls into a paranoid trance.

Gretchen, who looks extremely bored, leans over to Donnie.

GRETCHEN
Let's get out of here.

Donnie ignores her. His eyes are locked on Jim Cunningham, who begins his rousing re-enactment of the sad, unfortunate downfall of Frank.

Within minutes, Jim Cunningham has the crowd laughing . . . enamoured of him with his cartoon slide show.

Note: during this sequence the camera speed ramps to 4 fps.

INT. SCHOOL AUDITORIUM – NEXT (10:30 AM)

Donnie is in a trance.

DONNIE

We're moving through time.

GRETCHEN

What?

The huge screen rises upwards and Jim Cunningham takes questions from the crowd from portable mike stands in the back of the auditorium.

Several students get up and go to the mikes.

DORKY GIRL

Hi. Um . . . my stepsister . . . like . . . I sometimes worry that she eats too much.

OVERWEIGHT GIRL

(*mortified, yelling at her sister from the crowd*)

Shut up, Kim!

DORKY GIRL

I'm just trying to help you!

JIM CUNNINGHAM

There's no need to be embarrassed. Many times we eat because we are afraid to face the reality of our *ego reflection*. We shouldn't just look *into* the mirror. We should look *through* the mirror.

DORKY GIRL

Thanks.

Kitty Farmer runs out onto the stage and hands Jim Cunningham a bottle of water and a towel. She gives him the thumbs-up sign, and runs back offstage.

LANKY KID

Um . . . How can I decide what I want to be when I grow up?

JIM CUNNINGHAM

I think that you should look deep within yourself . . . deep within your heart . . . and find what it is in the world that makes you feel *love*. Just pure *love*. And then go to that. In your studies . . . in your athletics . . . go towards love.

Thank you.

Donnie gets up from his seat and goes to the mike.

LARRY RIESMAN

What can I do to learn how to fight?

JIM CUNNINGHAM

Violence is a product of fear. Those who love themselves enough should have no need to fight another person. Learn to truly love yourself . . . and the world will be yours.

LARRY RIESMAN

OK.

Donnie steps up to the mike stand.

DONNIE
(*furious*)
How much are they paying you to be here?

JIM CUNNINGHAM

Excuse me? What's your name, son?

DONNIE

Gerald.

JIM CUNNINGHAM

Well, Gerald, I think you're afraid.

DONNIE

Well, Jim . . . I think you're full of shit!

There are rumblings from the faculty. Some laughter from the student body.

Are you telling us this crap because you want us to buy your book? Because I'll tell you something, that was some of the worst advice that I've ever heard! (*to Dorky Girl*) If you want your sister to lose weight . . . tell her get off the couch, stop eating Twinkies . . . and maybe go out for field hockey. (*to Lanky Kid*) You're never gonna know what you want to be when you grow up. Most of the time, nobody does. How about you, Jim? (*to Larry*) And you . . . Sick of some jerk shoving your head in a toilet? Then go lift some weights . . . take a karate lesson. And when he tries to do it again . . . kick him in the balls.

More rumblings from the faculty . . . Laughter from the students gets louder.

> JIM CUNNINGHAM
> (*getting angry*)
> I think that you are afraid to ask me for advice. I think that you are a very troubled . . . confused young man. I think you're searching for answers in all the wrong places.

> DONNIE
> (*long beat*)
> Well, I think that you're the fucking Anti-Christ.

The crowd is stirring. Students break out into applause. Principal Cole approaches Donnie and removes him from the auditorium.

Gretchen watches him go with a smile.

EXT. OLD GUN ROAD – AFTERNOON (3:30 PM)

Donnie and Gretchen walk down the wooded road.

> DONNIE
> (*mumbling*)
> They suspended me for two days.

> GRETCHEN
> (*stopping him*)
> Are you OK?

> DONNIE
> (*long beat*)
> I've been seeing stuff . . . a lot of really messed-up stuff. (*Beat.*) Do you know who Grandma Death is?

> GRETCHEN
> Who?

> DONNIE
> The old crazy woman who lives off Old Gun Road.

Donnie takes out the book by Roberta Sparrow.

63

GRETCHEN

Oh yeah. (*taking the book*) *The Philosophy of Time Travel.*
What is this?

DONNIE

She wrote it. (*Beat.*) There are chapters in this book that
describe the stuff I've been seeing. It can't be just a coincidence.
(*Beat.*) Will you come see her with me?

EXT. OLD GUN ROAD – NEXT (3:45 PM)

*Donnie and Gretchen stand at the end of Grandma Death's
driveway.*

*Gretchen leads Donnie up to the front porch of the decrepit house.
She then rings the doorbell. They wait for several moments . . .
nothing happens.*

Gretchen then goes and peers through a window.

DONNIE

I know she's here. She never leaves the house.

GRETCHEN

Maybe she's asleep.

*They walk to the end of the driveway, and Donnie stops at the
mailbox. He opens it . . . empty.*

(*Pointing at the house.*) Donnie, look.

*In an upstairs window of the house, the silhouette of Grandma
Death peers down at them ominously.*

INT. DONNIE'S ROOM – AFTERNOON

Donnie sits at his desk, sealing an envelope. The address reads:

MS ROBERTA SPARROW
22 OLD GUN ROAD
MIDDLESEX, VA 23113

64

Title card:

OCTOBER 23 1988

INT. THERAPIST'S OFFICE – EVENING (6 PM)

Dr Thurman looks at a diagram from Sparrow's book. Donnie is pacing around her office.

> DR THURMAN
>
> And they grow out of our stomachs?

> DONNIE
>
> It was just like she described them in her book. Like they were alive. The way that they looked . . . moved . . . smelled. They were like workers . . . assigned to each one of us. (*Long beat, then distant.*) I followed my spear . . . and I found something . . .

> DR THURMAN
>
> What did you find?

Donnie is silent for a moment.

> DONNIE
>
> Nothing.

> DR THURMAN
>
> Have you told Gretchen about the spears?

> DONNIE
>
> Yeah, but if I told her about the other stuff about Frank . . .

> DR THURMAN
>
> Are you embarrassed by these things that you see?

> DONNIE
>
> You know . . . every week I come in here and I tell you stuff . . . and it's all embarrassing. I tell you stuff that I don't tell anyone else . . . and you know what? It's your turn, Dr Thurman. I'm not saying anything else until you tell me something embarrassing about yourself.

Donnie makes a 'zipper lip' gesture.

65

DR THURMAN
(*long, stubborn beat*)
I once had an extended sexual fantasy involving Mr Rogers.

Donnie just stares at her.

DONNIE
Whoa. (*Beat.*) That's OK, Dr Thurman it's nothing to be
embarrassed about. I have sexual fantasies all the time too.

DR THURMAN
I know.

DONNIE
I mean . . . Gretchen . . . She won't even let me kiss her. She
says because it's our first kiss . . . she's like waiting for this
big . . . moment or something. I just don't get it. I just want
to get it over with so we can move on to the good stuff.

DR THURMAN
The good stuff.

DONNIE
Yeah . . . you know . . . (*whispering*) fucking.

DR THURMAN
(*cutting him off*)
Have you ever made love, Donald?

Donnie looks at her . . . and we know the answer.

INT. KITCHEN – NIGHT (7:15 PM)

The entire family is having dinner. Donnie is lost in a trance.

SAMANTHA
Donnie, are you coming to my talent show tomorrow?

Donnie ignores her.

ROSE
He can't, Samantha. He's been suspended from after-school
activities. Donnie . . . are you still with us? (*Beat.*) How was
your therapy session tonight?

66

DONNIE

Fine. You know, Dr Thurman isn't so bad a lady. I can tell her anything.

Rose appears surprised and then sad at this comment. She looks at Eddie, who just looks down at his plate of food.

EXT. PHYSICS CLASS – DAY (12 PM)

Donnie and Gretchen are at the front on the stage presenting their invention. Dr Monnitoff presides.

DONNIE

So we call them . . . IMGs.

GRETCHEN

Infant Memory Generators.

DONNIE

Yeah. So the idea is that . . . you buy these glasses for your infant, and they wear them at night when they sleep.

GRETCHEN

And inside the glasses are these slide photographs. And each photograph is of something peaceful . . . or beautiful. Whatever pictures the parents want to put inside.

DR MONNITOFF

What effect do you think this would have on an infant?

DONNIE

Well . . . the thing is, nobody remembers their infancy. And anyone who says they do is lying. We think that this would help develop memory earlier in life.

DR MONNITOFF

Did you stop and think that maybe infants need darkness? That darkness is part of their natural development?

Seth Devlin raises his hand.

SETH

What if the parents like . . . put in photographs of Satan . . . pentagrams, dead people . . . stuff like that?

67

GRETCHEN

Is that what you'd show your kids?

SETH

I mean, didn't your dad like stab your mom?

Dr Monnitoff looks over at Seth calmly.

DR MONNITOFF

Get out.

Seth begins to walk out. Gretchen doesn't answer. There is only the 80 IQ grin . . . staring back at her face. The room is silent.

EXT. SCHOOL FRONT ENTRANCE – NEXT (2:15 PM)

Gretchen walks out the front door. Donnie comes chasing after her.

DONNIE

Gretchen! Gretchen . . . wait up!

She turns and faces him . . . tears in her eyes.

I'm so sorry.

They embrace . . . kissing for the first time.

EXT. BYRD THEATRE – MAGIC HOUR (5:30 PM)

The old-fashioned theatre marquee reads:

HALLOWEEN FRIGHTMARE
THE EVIL DEAD / THE LAST TEMPTATION OF CHRIST

Donnie and Gretchen approach the box office.

DONNIE

Two for *Evil Dead*, please.

INT. BYRD THEATRE – NEXT

Donnie and Gretchen sit in the middle of the huge, empty theatre.

The Evil Dead unfolds. They eat popcorn and watch silently. Donnie looks over and sees that Gretchen is asleep.

Donnie turns back to the movie . . . beginning to look ill.

FRANK

Feeling sick?

Donnie turns his head over and looks across Gretchen. Frank is sitting next to her.

I want to show you something.

DONNIE

You have to do something for me first.

FRANK

You have a request?

DONNIE

Yeah. Tell me why you're wearing that stupid bunny suit.

FRANK

Why are you wearing that stupid man suit?

DONNIE

Take it off. I want to see you.

After a moment, Frank slowly reaches up and removes the rabbit headpiece.

Donnie's eyes widen.

Underneath the headpiece is the human face of a handsome young man. His left eye does not exist, because it has imploded into the socket. There is blood oozing from the wound.

FRANK

Satisfied?

Donnie just stares at him.

DONNIE

What happened to your eye?

FRANK

I am so sorry.

DONNIE

Why do they call you Frank?

FRANK

It is the name of my father . . . and his father before me.

69

DONNIE

How much longer is this gonna last?

FRANK

You should already know that. (*Beat.*) Watch the movie,
Donnie. I have something to show you.

Donnie looks at the screen.

On the screen, The Evil Dead *morphs into a Time Portal.*

There's a storm coming. (*Beat.*) Have you ever seen a Portal,
Donnie?

Suddenly . . . the screen morphs to an image of a large Tudor house.

Burn it to the ground.

Donnie pulls out Jim Cunningham's wallet from his pocket.

*Donnie contemplates his fate for several more moments, and then
gets up and walks out.*

EXT. BYRD THEATRE – NIGHT (6:30 PM)

Donnie walks slowly past the theatre marquee.

INT. AUDITORIUM – NIGHT (7 PM)

*On the stage, among blowing autumn leaves, Cherita Chen performs
a strangely beautiful mime act to Symphony No. 3 by Henryk Gorecki.*

*When her act is finally over, the crowd is indifferent, with scattered
applause and laughter. Ms Pomeroy stands up and applauds
enthusiastically.*

Clearly affected by the laughter, Cherita walks offstage.

In the front row, the entire Darko family has assembled.

INT. AUDITORIUM BACKSTAGE – NIGHT (7:15 PM)

Kitty Farmer stands with the five-member dance team in a huddle.

MS FARMER

Now girls . . . I want you to concentrate. Failure is not an
option. And Bethany . . . if you feel the need to vomit up there.
Just swallow it.

BETH

OK, Mom.

Jim Cunningham walks past them towards the stage. He stops and touches Samantha on the shoulder . . . smiling.

JIM CUNNINGHAM

Good luck out there.

She smiles nervously back at him. He exits onto the stage.

INT. AUDITORIUM STAGE – NEXT (7:20 PM)

JIM CUNNINGHAM

Thank you . . . Cherita Chen. That was Autumn Angel. (*clearing his throat*) Next . . . it is my distinct pleasure to introduce to you . . . Emily Bates . . . Suzy Bailey . . . Samantha Darko . . . Beth Farmer . . . and Joanie James. They are . . . SPARKLE MOTION!

The audience roars with applause as the lights dim.

The following montage alternates between the auditorium stage and Jim Cunningham's house.

The stage lights slowly raise as the opening beat of 'West End Girls' by the Pet Shop Boys begins.

Under the soft stage lights . . . Sparkle Motion unfolds.

Donnie approaches Jim Cunningham's house.

Sparkle Motion . . . in perfect synchronicity.

In the living room of the house . . . Donnie walks through, dousing gasoline all over the place with psychotic force. A trail of fire spreads.

A mystery woman emerges from the back wall of the auditorium.

A couch and curtains become engulfed in flames.

Middlesex girls are jumping up and down in the aisles.

Eddie and Rose are smiling ear to ear.

Elizabeth Darko is cracking up at the entire scene.

Kids are going bonkers in the aisles.

71

The mystery woman takes off her glasses.

Slow motion: fire engulfs a deer taxidermy.

Ms Pomeroy gets into the groove.

The parents are now on their feet.

The crowd roars even louder.

Slow motion: Sparkle Motion stands triumphant.

Slow motion: Donnie stands before a wall of flames.

EXT. SCHOOL AUDITORIUM – NIGHT (8 PM)

Cherita sits alone in the courtyard at the base of the mongrel statue . . . defeated and alone.

INT. BYRD THEATRE – NIGHT (9 PM)

Donnie walks into the theatre and sits next to Gretchen, who is asleep. As the credits to the film roll, Donnie wakes her.

> GRETCHEN
> What? (*disoriented*) How long was I asleep?

> DONNIE
> The whole movie. Let's go.

INT. JIM CUNNINGHAM'S HOUSE – NIGHT (9:45 PM)

Firemen walk through the charred room shining flashlights.

A Fireman shines his flashlight onto a mysterious door with smoke emerging from it.

He kicks the door in . . . and shines the flashlight into the dark hole.

EXT. CARPATHIAN RIDGE – SUNRISE (5 AM)

Donnie and Gretchen lie awake on a pile of blankets . . . staring out into the abyssal canyon.

Helicopter shot: we swoop down over Carpathian Ridge . . . past Donnie and Gretchen . . . over the canyon and the endless expanse of evergreen forest.

Title card:

OCTOBER 22 1988

EXT. DARKO HOUSE BACKYARD/PATIO – MORNING (11 AM)

Donnie and Eddie are in the back yard raking leaves onto a giant sheet.

> DONNIE
>
> I know everyone thinks I'm a nutcase. I've been getting a lot of weird looks from people lately.

They rake in silence for a moment.

> EDDIE
> (*angry*)
> Who's been giving you weird looks?

> DONNIE
>
> A lot of people. Teachers. Younger kids. It's like they are afraid of me for some reason. (*Beat.*) But that's OK . . . because I know I deserve it.

Eddie stops raking.

> EDDIE
>
> You're my only son . . .

> DONNIE
>
> I know, Dad.

> EDDIE
>
> I know I'm not the best . . . communicator. (*Beat.*) But whatever happens in your life . . . whatever obstacles you come up against . . . you just say . . . and do whatever is in your heart. You be honest . . . and tell the truth . . . even if they look at you funny . . . and they will. They'll tell you that you're wrong. They'll call you a fool. (*Beat.*) But what you've got to understand, son, is that almost all of those people are full of shit. They're all part of this great big conspiracy of bullshit . . . and they're scared of people like you. Because you're smarter than all of them.

Donnie smiles at his father.

INT. DONNIE'S ROOM – AFTERNOON (1 PM)

Donnie sits on his bed and stares at the calendar on his wall. Each day is marked with an X.

He takes his pills from his nightstand . . . and downs three.

There are noises coming from downstairs.

INT. FAMILY ROOM – AFTERNOON

Donnie comes downstairs to see Elizabeth glued to the TV.

ELIZABETH
Oh my God, that's him. That's the guy from last night.

On the television: a Newscaster stands in front of the charred heap of what was once a large suburban house. Firefighters mill about behind her.

NEWSCASTER
As firefighters continue their investigation, arson has not been ruled out as the cause of the fire, particularly because of the shocking discovery made earlier today among the burned ruins. In the basement of the house authorities have discovered what has been described as a kiddie-porn dungeon.

Policemen emerge from the basement with several large boxes of evidence.

Cunningham, who has become a recent celebrity for his motivational books, audio tapes and videos, ducked his head from cameras when he was arrested at the Sarasota Heights Golf Club this morning. In a vicious statement, Cunning Visions executive Linda Connie attacked the Middlesex Fire Department . . . claiming a vast conspiracy.

Donnie stares at the television . . . speechless, horrified. On the TV Jim Cunningham hides his face from the camera.

ELIZABETH
Oh my God. Dad played golf with that guy.

Donnie says nothing, turns around . . . and walks upstairs.

Donnie and Dr Monnitoff are having another in-depth conversation.

DR MONNITOFF
Each vessel travels along a vector path through space–time . . .
along its centre of gravity.

DONNIE
(*to himself*)
Like a spear.

DR MONNITOFF
Beg pardon?

DONNIE
Like a spear that comes out of your stomach?

DR MONNITOFF
Uhh . . . sure. And in order for the vessel to travel through time
it must find the *portal*, in this case the wormhole, or some
unforeseen portal that lies undiscovered.

DONNIE
Could these wormholes appear in nature?

DR MONNITOFF
That . . . is highly unlikely. You're talking about an act of God.

DONNIE
If God controls time . . . then all time is pre-decided. Then
every living thing travels along a set path.

DR MONNITOFF
I'm not following you.

DONNIE
If you could see your path or channel growing out of your
stomach you could see into the future. And that's a form of
time travel, right?

DR MONNITOFF
You are contradicting yourself, Donnie. If we could see our
destinies manifest themselves visually . . . then we would be
given the *choice* to *betray our chosen destinies*. The very fact

75

that this *choice* would exist . . . would mean that all *preformed destiny* would end.

> DONNIE
> Not if you *chose* to stay within God's channel . . .

> DR MONNITOFF
> (*cutting him off*)
> Donnie, I'm afraid I can't continue this conversation. I could lose my job.

INT. TEACHER'S LOUNGE – AFTERNOON (2:30 PM)

Ms Pomeroy sits across from Dr Monnitoff. They both grade papers silently.

Dr Monnitoff stares at her for a long moment.

> DR MONNITOFF
> (*incredulous*)
> Donnie . . . Darko.

She stares at him for a while . . . haunted by something.

INT. PRINCIPAL COLE'S OFFICE – AFTERNOON (3 PM)

Ms Pomeroy sits across from Principal Cole.

> PRINCIPAL COLE
> I'm sorry, Karen, this is a specialised school. We don't think the methods you've undertaken here are appropriate.

> MS POMEROY
> Appropriate. (*trying to contain her anger*) With all due respect, sir, what specifically is it about my methods you find inappropriate?

Principal Cole stares at her for a moment.

> PRINCIPAL COLE
> I don't have time to get into a debate about this, Karen, I believe I have made myself clear.

> MS POMEROY
> You call this . . . clarity? I don't think you have a clue what it's really like to communicate with these kids. You don't think

that they can smell your bullshit from a mile away? Every day that goes by . . . that we fail to . . . inspire them . . . is another moment that we all lose. And we are losing them to apathy, and this . . . prescribed nonsense. They are slipping away . . .

PRINCIPAL COLE

I am sorry that you have failed. Now if you'll excuse me I have another appointment. You can finish out the week.

INT. SCHOOL OFFICE/TEACHERS' LOUNGE – NEXT (3:15 PM)

Ms Pomeroy steps out from Principal Cole's office. She sees Kitty Farmer and the Sparkle Motion girls milling about. The mystery woman is there as well.

Ms Pomeroy glares at Kitty Farmer before leaving.

EXT. MIDDLESEX RIDGE SCHOOL – NEXT (3:30 PM)

Ms Pomeroy steps outside through an emergency exit. She stares out at the beautiful forest. Her eyes are filled with tears.

MS POMEROY

FUUUUUUUCKKKKKKK!!!!!

Hearing the scream from the distance, we see Cherita Chen turn her head in shock as she walks alone along the edge of the school building . . . eating her lunch.

She and Ms Pomeroy share a moment of eye contact before she turns and heads back into the school.

INT. MAIN SCHOOL HALLWAY – NEXT (3:45 PM)

Ms Pomeroy walks slowly through the hallway, wiping tears from her face.

PRINCIPAL COLE
(*over the intercom*)

Good afternoon. It is my great pleasure to announce that the Middlesex Middle School dance team has been invited to perform on Ed McMahon's Star Search '88 in Los Angeles, California . . .

INT. PRINCIPAL COLE'S OFFICE – NEXT (3:45 PM)

The Sparkle Motion girls squeal with excitement . . . jumping up and down. Kitty Farmer pumps her fist in victory.

Suddenly . . . Linda Connie bursts into the office, grabbing Kitty by the arm. The teacher holds up a newspaper . . . where there is a headline that reads: JIM CUNNINGHAM CHARGED.

Kitty's facial expression goes from elation to horror.

INT. ENGLISH CLASS – MORNING (8:30 AM)

The classroom is dark. The students watch Watership Down, *the movie.*

Donnie is asleep. Gretchen stares at him. Ms Pomeroy stares at Gretchen.

Suddenly, she turns on the lights, turning off the TV.

Donnie wakes up . . . with dark circles under his eyes.

> MS POMEROY
> And when the other rabbits hear of Fiver's vision, do they believe him? (*Coughs.*) It could be the death of an entire way of life, the end of an era.

> DONNIE
> Why should we care?

> MS POMEROY
> Because the rabbits are us, Donnie.

> DONNIE
> Why should I mourn for a rabbit like it was human?

> MS POMEROY
> Is the death of one species less tragic than another?

> DONNIE
> Of course. A rabbit is not like us. It has no history books . . . it has no knowledge of sorrow or regret. It has no photographs . . . no mirrors. I mean, don't get me wrong. I like bunnies and all. They're cute . . . and they're horny. And if you're cute and horny . . . then you're probably happy that you don't know

78

who you are . . . or why you're even alive. But the only thing
I've known rabbits to do is have sex as many times as possible
before they die.

He looks over at Gretchen, who looks angry at this.

There's no point in crying for a dead rabbit . . . who never
feared death to begin with.

The class is silent for a moment.

> GRETCHEN
> You're wrong. (*Beat.*) You're wrong about these rabbits. These
> rabbits can talk. They are the product of the author's imagination.
> And he cares for them. So we care for them too. We care that
> their home has been destroyed . . . and that their lives are in
> danger. Otherwise . . . we've missed the point.

> MS POMEROY
> But aren't we forgetting the miracle of storytelling? The *dea ex
> machina*. The god machine. That is how the rabbits are saved.

*Gretchen looks across the room at Donnie with a disdainful
expression.*

INT. MAIN SCHOOL HALLWAY – LATER (9 AM)

Donnie approaches Gretchen at her locker.

> DONNIE
> You want to skip fourth period and go to the Ridge?

> GRETCHEN
> (*angry*)
> What's wrong with you?

> DONNIE
> What do you mean?

She turns and walks off, leaving Donnie broken and dejected.

INT. DONNIE'S ROOM – NIGHT (6:30 PM)

*Donnie sits at his desk looking at an intricate drawing of a cloud
formation. On it he has written:* THE PORTAL.

INT. KITCHEN – NIGHT (7 PM)

Rose and Eddie are in the kitchen. He is getting ready for a business trip.

Samantha is jumping up and down. Elizabeth is jumping up and down, dancing with her.

Donnie looks into the kitchen from the foyer, catching his family in a serene, contented moment of happiness. A moment that he chooses not to interrupt.

Title card:

OCTOBER 25 1988

INT./EXT. FOYER/FRONT PORCH – DAY (3 PM)

Doorbell rings. Rose answers the door.

Kitty Farmer is there on the front porch. She is wearing a T-shirt that reads: GOD IS AWESOME!

> MS FARMER

Rose.

> ROSE

Kitty . . .

> MS FARMER

Rose, we have a crisis. (*Beat.*) I am sure that you are aware of the horrible allegations against Jim Cunningham.

> ROSE

Yes, I saw the news. Something about a kiddie-porn dungeon

> MS FARMER
> (*holding up her hand*)

Please! Don't say those words. (*shaking her head*) Well . . . as you can see . . . many of us are devastated by this news. This is obviously some kind of conspiracy meant to destroy an innocent man. And I have taken it upon myself to spearhead the Jim Cunningham defence campaign. But unfortunately my civic duties have created a conflict of interest . . . which involves you.

ROSE

Beg pardon?

MS FARMER

Rose . . . I have to appear at his arraignment tomorrow
morning. And as you know, the girls also leave for Los Angeles
tomorrow morning. Now, as their coach . . . I was the obvious
choice to chaperone them on the trip.

ROSE

But now you can't go.

MS FARMER

Yes. And believe me, of all the other mothers I would never
dream of asking you, given the predicament with your son. But
none of the other mothers are able to go.

ROSE

Oh, Kitty, I don't know. This is so last-minute . . . Eddie is in
New York . . .

MS FARMER

Rose . . . I don't know if you realise how great an opportunity
this is for our daughters. This has been a dream of ours for
a long time. (*Beat.*) Sometimes I doubt your commitment to
Sparkle Motion.

INT. DONNIE'S ROOM – NIGHT (7 PM)

*Rose is standing in Donnie's room alone. She stares at a drawing of
Frank that he has tacked onto his bulletin board.*

Donnie appears in the doorway. Rose jumps.

DONNIE

I feel like . . . I'm approaching something horrible.

*Donnie walks over and sits on his bed. Rose goes and sits next to
him.*

ROSE

I have to take the girls to Los Angeles tomorrow.

DONNIE

Do you get to meet Ed?

81

ROSE

If I'm lucky. (*Beat.*) So . . . I won't be back until the first. Your dad will be back on Sunday, so I've put Elizabeth in charge until then. She has the car . . . so she can drive you to your therapy tomorrow.

DONNIE

How does it feel to have a wacko for a son?

ROSE
(*embracing him*)

It feels wonderful.

EXT. DARKO HOUSE DRIVEWAY – MORNING (10 AM)

Rose brings her luggage out to the airport van. Mystery Woman loads Beth Farmer into the van.

Donnie sits on the back-porch steps, watching everyone silently. Elizabeth gives Samantha a hug.

ELIZABETH

You're gonna win. I know it.

SAMANTHA

So do I. (*to Donnie*) Bye, Donnie.

Donnie waves goodbye.

ROSE

Here are the keys to the Taurus. There's plenty of groceries in the fridge. And I left money on the kitchen table. And don't forget . . .

ELIZABETH

Don't worry, Mom. Just go, you'll miss your flight.

Rose turns . . . wanting to say goodbye to Donnie, but not knowing how. She smiles and waves goodbye.

Donnie waves back.

Rose turns and goes to the van . . . handing the driver her last bag.

DONNIE

Mom . . .

Donnie stands up, and reluctantly approaches from the porch.

There's nothing broken . . . in my brain.

Rose stands there for a moment looking at her only son.

SAMANTHA

Come on, Mom!

ROSE
(to Donnie, holding back tears)

I know.

She gets into the van, as Donnie and Elizabeth watch them drive off.

INT. SCHOOL MAIN HALLWAY – AFTERNOON (3 PM)

Donnie walks up to Gretchen . . . who stands at her locker with several other girls. The girls whisper to each other as she approaches.

DONNIE

Will you please talk to me?

GRETCHEN

Not now, Donnie. It isn't a good time.

DONNIE

Then when? I have to talk to you.

Gretchen walks away, looking back at him with apologetic eyes.

INT. ENGLISH CLASS – MOMENTS LATER (3:15 PM)

Donnie walks alone through the hallways . . . lost.

He stumbles upon Ms Pomeroy's room. She sits behind her desk . . . which has been packed up into a cardboard box.

DONNIE
(knocking on the door)

Ms Pomeroy . . . what's going on?

MS POMEROY

Donnie . . . it's Friday. Shouldn't you be off with your friends, scaring old people?

83

DONNIE

Where are you going?

MS POMEROY

I don't know. That's a good question . . . but suffice it to say
that I am no longer your English teacher. They fired me.

DONNIE

That's bullshit. You're a good teacher.

MS POMEROY

Thank you, Donnie. And you're a good student. Lazy . . . but
a good student. Unlike most of the others, you question Mom
and Dad's rules.

DONNIE

What do I tell the rest of the class when they ask about you?

MS POMEROY
(*long beat*)

Tell them that everything is going to be just fine. (*Beat.*) It is
up to the children to save themselves these days. Because the
parents . . . they don't have a clue.

*Donnie looks at the blackboard. On it she has written in perfect
penmanship: 'Cellar Door'.*

DONNIE

What's . . . Cellar Door?

MS POMEROY
(*spaced out*)

A famous linguist once said . . . that of all the phrases in the
English language, of all the endless combinations of words in
all of history . . . that 'Cellar Door' is the most beautiful.

She is silent for a moment.

DONNIE

Cellar Door.

MS POMEROY

Sometimes it's the only thing that keeps us going.

She takes the box, and crosses the room towards Donnie.

So . . . will Donnie Darko find his Cellar Door?

DONNIE

I think I already have. (*Beat.*) But now she won't even talk to
me.

MS POMEROY

Then go find her, Donnie. Don't let her get away. (*stopping at
the door*) She was right about the rabbits. Go.

INT. MAIN HALLWAY – NEXT (3:15 PM)

*And with that . . . Ms Pomeroy turns and walks down the hallway
with her career in a cardboard box . . . heading towards the bright
Friday afternoon sunlight.*

*Donnie walks back down the hallway . . . lost in his own
introspection.*

*Across the way . . . at her locker . . . is Cherita Chen. Donnie
approaches her slowly like a cat.*

She turns from her locker . . . and they make eye contact.

*She looks at him warily, frightened. A book falls from her arms onto
the floor.*

Written in large letters on the brown book cover is his name:

DONNIE DARKO

*He comes face to face with her, grabs her earmuffs with both hands,
and touches his forehead to hers as if he were going to kiss her.*

DONNIE
(*long beat*)
I promise that one day things will get better for you.

*Cherita holds still for a moment, trembling, and then jerks back
from him. Her earmuffs come off in his hands.*

She backs away from him slowly. A single tear rolls down her cheek.

CHERITA

Chut . . . up!

She then turns and runs down the hall . . . disappearing from sight.

85

EXT. OLD GUN ROAD – AFTERNOON (4 PM)

Donnie walks by himself . . . thinking . . . wearing Cherita's earmuffs.

Title card:

OCTOBER 29 1988

INT. THERAPIST'S OFFICE – DAY (1:30 PM)

Donnie is under hypnosis.

> DR THURMAN
> And when I clap my hands together twice, you will wake up.
> Do you understand?

> DONNIE
> Yes.

> DR THURMAN
> So your parents . . . why did you disappoint them?

> DONNIE
> I . . . I was playing with fire.

> DR THURMAN
> Is it Frank who wants you to destroy the world, to set the
> world on fire?

Donnie doesn't answer.

> DONNIE
> People get hurt.

> DR THURMAN
> But it was an accident. The house was under construction.

> DONNIE
> People get hurt. I don't want to hurt anyone.

> DR THURMAN
> But you were punished.

> DONNIE
> Yes. I went to jail.

> DR THURMAN
> Do you wish that you were punished by your parents instead?

86

They . . . didn't buy me what I wanted for Christmas that year.

What did you want for Christmas that year?

Hungry Hungry Hippos.

How did you feel . . . being denied these Hungry Hungry Hippos?

Regret.

What else makes you feel regret?

That I did it again.

(*alarmed*)

You've done it again?

Yes. I flooded my school . . . and I burned down that pervert's house. I think I only have a few days left . . . before they catch me.

Why did you do these things, Donnie? Did Frank tell you to commit these crimes?

He does not respond.

I have to obey him . . . because he saved my life. He controls me and I have to obey him or I'll be left all alone . . . and I'll never figure out what all of this means . . .

If God exists?

I think now that he might . . .

DR THURMAN

Why?

DONNIE

Because I'm so horny.

DR THURMAN

God exists because you're horny.

DONNIE

I think so. I think that's one of the clues. It's a clue that tells
us . . . to keep going.

DR THURMAN

Where are we going?

No answer.

Where are we going, Donald?

DONNIE

I have the power to build a time machine.

DR THURMAN

How is that possible?

DONNIE

Grandma Death will teach me how. Soon.

DR THURMAN

Then how is time travel possible?

DONNIE

It would have to be God's portal. They will lead me to it. Then
I will go back in time . . . and I won't feel regret any more.

DR THURMAN

When will this happen?

DONNIE

Soon. Time is almost up.

*Donnie gets up on his feet staggering around the room. He looks
frightened . . . childlike.*

It has to happen soon . . . it has to happen soon.

Dr Thurman gets up and tries to control Donnie . . . following him around the room.

> DR THURMAN
> What is going to happen?

> DONNIE
> *(freaking out)*
> Frank is going to kill.

> DR THURMAN
> Who is he going to kill?

Dr Thurman grabs him, trying to get him under control in an awkward embrace.

> Who is he going to kill?

Donnie stares across the office like a frightened child . . . as the room becomes white with artificial light.

Frank is there in the office . . . staring back at him.

> DONNIE
> *(freaking out)*
> I can see him right now!

> DR THURMAN
> Where is he, Donald?

> DONNIE
> He's right there . . . He can read my mind and he'll show me the way out of this. The sky is going to open up . . . and then He will reveal himself to me.

> DR THURMAN
> If the sky were suddenly to open up . . . there would be no law . . . there would be no rule. There would only be you and your memories . . . the choices you've made and the people you've touched. The life that has been carved out from your subconscious is the only evidence by which you will be judged . . . by which you must judge yourself. Because when this world ends there will only be you and him . . . and no one else.

> DONNIE
> It's too late. I've already ruined my whole life.

DR THURMAN

You will survive this . . . Donald. I promise you that you will survive. You must let me help you. (*Beat.*) And when I clap my hands together you will wake up.

She claps her hands together twice . . . and Donnie snaps out of his trance.

INT. THERAPIST'S OFFICE – AFTERNOON (2 PM)

Donnie, calmed down and putting his jacket on, walks slowly to the doorway.

Dr Thurman stands looking out the window.

DR THURMAN

Donald?

Donnie turns back and faces her. Beat.

Your medication. They're placebos. Just pills made of water.

DONNIE

Thank you.

DR THURMAN

Donald, an atheist is someone who denies altogether the existence of a God. You are an agnostic. An agnostic is someone who believes that there can be no proof of the existence of God . . . but does not deny the possibility that God exists.

DONNIE

Goodbye, Dr Thurman.

DR THURMAN

Goodbye, Donald.

INT. KITCHEN – DAY

Donnie walks into the kitchen, where Elizabeth is sitting at the table.

ELIZABETH
(*in shock*)

I got in. I'm going to Harvard.

DONNIE

Congratulations.

Donnie sits down across from her.

> Mom and Dad won't be back until Sunday night. It's Halloween Carnival. We should throw a party. We could totally get away with it.

ELIZABETH
(long beat)

> OK, but it has to be a small one.

DONNIE

> Everything is going to be just fine.

INT. FOYER — NIGHT (9 PM)

EXT. DARKO HOUSE — NIGHT (9 PM)

Neighbourhood kids are trick-or-treating. The man in the red jogging suit shines a flashlight towards the house.

There are at least two dozen cars parked in front . . . and somebody is already throwing toilet paper in the trees.

INT. FOYER — NIGHT (9:30 PM)

The doorbell rings. Donnie answers the door . . . only to find Sean and Ronald dressed in black with monster masks. They are both carrying backpacks.

Donnie is dressed in a black skeleton suit, and his face is painted white like a skull.

SEAN

> We got eggs, water balloons and a dozen rolls of toilet paper.

RONALD

> I stole four beers from my dad.

DONNIE

> There's a keg here.

SEAN

> Only pussies drink keg beer.

They go back into the house towards the kitchen. There are at least forty people, already quite wasted, many carrying their own twelve-packs of beer under their arms.

Almost everyone is wearing a costume. Donnie and his friends weave through the crowd towards the patio.

EXT. BACKYARD/PATIO – NEXT

Donnie and his friends watching the party unfold.

The party grows larger.

INT. THERAPIST'S OFFICE – NIGHT

Dr Thurman paces around her office with the phone to her ear.

INT. MASTER BEDROOM – NIGHT

The phone is ringing. The answering machine picks up.

INT. FOYER – LATER ON (11 PM)

The doorbell rings . . . and once again Donnie is the one to answer it. To his surprise . . . it is Gretchen standing on his front porch.

> GRETCHEN
> (*very upset*)

Hey.

> DONNIE

Hey. You OK?

> GRETCHEN
> (*walking inside*)

My mom is gone.

> DONNIE

Where is she?

> GRETCHEN
> (*close to tears*)

I don't know. She didn't leave a note. The house is all messed up.

> DONNIE

But you're OK?

She nods yes.

Did you call the cops?

GRETCHEN
Yeah, they told me to get out of the house.

Donnie takes Gretchen into the hallway and gives her a hug.

I'm so scared . . . I just keep thinking that something awful has happened. It's my fucking stepdad. I know it.

DONNIE
(*embraces her*)
It's safe here.

Donnie takes Gretchen upstairs. We reveal Elizabeth watching them go.

INT. FAMILY ROOM – NEXT

Elizabeth walks over to a friend.

ELIZABETH
(*yelling over the music*)
Have you seen Frank?

FRIEND
No, I think they said they were going on a beer run.

INT. MASTER BEDROOM – NEXT (11:15 PM)

Donnie and Gretchen sit on the bed. Gretchen takes a sip of beer.

GRETCHEN
Some people are just born with tragedy in their blood.

He kisses her. He then pulls back.

What?

DONNIE
There's something you have to know, Gretchen. (*Beat.*)
Everything is going to be just fine.

They lie down together . . . silently listening to the party below.

93

The phone is ringing. The answering machine picks up.

ROSE

(on the answering machine)

If you're there, please pick up. (*Beat.*) Oh well . . . there's good news. The girls . . . they got three and a half stars . . . and they get to come back for the quarter-finals.

INT. LAX TERMINAL – NIGHT (9 PM PST)

Rose stands at a payphone while the Sparkle Motion girls wait at the terminal.

SAMANTHA

Semi-finals, Mom!

ROSE

Sorry . . . semi-finals. Anyway . . . we're taking the red-eye back tonight and we should arrive around six a.m. I hope everything is alright. Bye.

INT. FOYER – NIGHT (12 AM)

We move towards the grandfather clock and see the minute hand reach midnight.

INT. FOYER – NIGHT (12:30 AM)

Donnie and Gretchen walk downstairs. They kiss, and she goes towards the family room.

Donnie walks towards the kitchen, but then doubles over against the wall in pain.

Suddenly . . . the room blows out with a strobe of white light . . . as costumed teenagers and their vector spears intersect in a shimmering maze of chaos.

Donnie slowly follows his spear as it leads him through the crowd . . . directly towards the refrigerator.

Donnie stares blankly at what he sees . . . scrawled in magic marker on the memo board.

It reads: FRANK WAS HERE . . . WENT TO GET BEER!!

Donnie stares at the board for several moments . . . he then turns his head and sees a teenager with a Ronald Reagan mask walk by. He then sees another spear come towards him. Gretchen rounds the corner, coming in from the family room.

Donnie falls to his knees and puts his face inside the end of Gretchen's spear. We see his POV: an abyssal tunnel of light.

Donnie stands up, coming face to face with Gretchen.

> DONNIE

Come with me.

> GRETCHEN

Where are we going?

He grabs her and pulls her out the back of the kitchen into the back yard. Ronald and Sean follow.

EXT. BACKYARD/PATIO – NEXT

They move through the back yard.

> GRETCHEN

Donnie, what's going on!

She stops him.

> DONNIE

Time is running out. We have to go see Grandma Death. We have to talk to her.

> GRETCHEN

Why? Is this about the book?

> DONNIE

No. Frank.

> GRETCHEN

Who is Frank?

Ronald and Sean approach.

> SEAN

Donnie? Where are we going?

Donnie looks at Gretchen . . . This is it.

DONNIE

She knows. I know she knows.

EXT. NEIGHBOURHOOD STREET – NIGHT (1:15 AM)

The group of four ride their bikes down the street.

EXT. FOREST – NIGHT (1:45 AM)

They ride their bikes through the forest.

EXT. GRANDMA DEATH'S HOUSE – NIGHT (1:30 AM)

They stand in front of the dark house. It is pitch-black. No lights anywhere.

SEAN

There's nobody here . . . Just forget it.

Then . . . there is a clanking noise from somewhere around the side of the house. Everyone hears it.

Donnie looks towards the lower front of the house where there is a cellar door.

GRETCHEN

Is that a cellar door?

DONNIE
(his eyes widen)

Yeah . . .

The cellar door is ajar . . . and there is a dim light coming out from inside.

RONALD

Don't open it, Donnie. Let's just leave.

INT. GRANDMA DEATH'S CELLAR – NEXT

Donnie and Gretchen open the door to the cellar . . . and descend down into a murky pit with a stone floor.

Inside . . . the room is quite large . . . filled with row after row of boxes, paintings, antique furniture and chandeliers. There is even an ancient piano in the back.

Gretchen slowly reaches her hand out and places her finger on the deepest piano key.

Suddenly, a figure emerges from the shadows and slams Donnie into the wall. He then grabs Gretchen by placing an arm around her neck with a butcher's knife.

It is Ricky Danforth. Seth comes out from another corner . . . also brandishing a butcher's knife. Both have pantyhose pulled over their heads.

RICKY

Get the fuck out! Now!

Ricky drags Gretchen out. Seth drags Donnie out.

EXT. GRANDMA DEATH'S HOUSE – NEXT

The four of them come bursting out of the cellar.

Seth holds Donnie's arms down with his knees and places the butcher's knife against his throat.

Ricky throws Gretchen down hard onto the shoulder of Old Gun Road. She lets out a gasp of pain as her head hits the gravel.

RICKY

Motherfuckers!

SETH

I have . . . a bigger knife now.

Sean and Ronald watch . . . dumbfounded . . . backing away.

Seth just stares down at Donnie with his dead eyes . . . pushing the knife down harder, cutting off Donnie's air supply.

SEAN

Hey . . . there's someone coming! Look, there's a car coming!

Seth slowly turns his head and sees . . . far down Old Gun Road . . . approaching headlights.

DONNIE
(barely audible whisper)

Dea ex machina . . .

What did you say?

Our saviour . . .

The headlights are getting closer.

They called the fuckin' cops!

Gretchen struggles to breathe on the shoulder of the road . . . the wind knocked out of her, semi-conscious.

That's no cop . . .

The headlights are getting closer.

(in a hoarse whisper)

Donnie . . .

Even closer . . .

You better run.

Forget it . . . let's go!

Seth doesn't move . . . He just stares down at Donnie.

Come on! Let's go!

You're dead, Donnie Darko.

Seth gets up and runs off with Ricky into the forest . . . just as the approaching car crests the top of Old Gun Road at breakneck speed.

Suddenly, in the bright glow of the car's headlights . . . is the silhouette of Grandma Death . . . standing in the middle of the road. In her right hand she is clutching a letter.

Donnie's letter.

Donnie . . .

The car swerves left . . . barely missing Grandma Death.

The Pontiac tries to brake hard . . . but the wheels lock . . . and it goes skidding onto the shoulder.

Gretchen raises her head from the gravel . . . into bright headlight beams.

The Trans-Am goes barrelling over her like a speed-bump . . . and her limp body rolls off into the grassy ditch.

The Trans-Am skids off into the grass and collides head-on with the crumbling stone chimney . . . which explodes into the crumpled hood of the car . . . as it eventually comes to a stop in a fury of smoke.

Donnie staggers to his feet . . . regaining his breath. He runs over to Gretchen and kneels down next to her.

DONNIE
Gretchen . . . wake up. Wake up.

Her neck is broken. She has no pulse.

The passenger door to the Trans-Am opens, and a passenger in a clown costume gets out.

The driver's side door opens and the driver gets out.

He is wearing a rabbit suit. A Halloween costume.

He is holding the grotesque rabbit helmet in his hand.

It is Frank.

PASSENGER
Frank . . . what'd you do . . . what'd you do!

Frank approaches Donnie . . . who raises his head from Gretchen to see him for the first time . . . face to face . . . with an expression of shocked horror.

She's dead! You killed her, Frank!

Frank is in shock.

FRANK
She's dead.

Donnie slowly nods his head. Sean and Ronald approach him slowly. Grandma Death looms behind them.

What the fuck. Look at my fucking car!

99

PASSENGER

Let's get out of here. Let's get out of here, Frank!

FRANK

What were you stupid fucks doing in the middle of the road?

DONNIE

Waiting for you.

Donnie raises the gun from his father's closet with his right hand, and to his own surprise, he pulls the trigger.

Frank's left eye implodes as the bullet passes through his head. His body falls limply to the ground.

PASSENGER

Holy shit . . .

The Passenger turns and runs off into the woods.

RONALD

What'd you do, Donnie? What'd you do!

DONNIE
(*very calm*)

Go home. Go home and tell your parents that everything is going to be just fine.

After contemplation of the recent events . . . Sean and Ronald turn and run off in the opposite direction.

Donnie is left alone . . . with the dead bodies.

He turns and stares at Grandma Death . . . who is calmly standing there . . . with his letter in her hand.

GRANDMA DEATH

A storm is coming. (*Beat.*) You must hurry.

Donnie is still in shock.

EXT. NEIGHBOURHOOD STREET – EARLY MORNING (4:30 AM)

Donnie carries Gretchen home.

100

INT. FAMILY ROOM – NEXT

Donnie looks down at Elizabeth on the couch. He then leans down and gives her a kiss on the forehead.

EXT. DARKO HOUSE DRIVEWAY – NEXT

Donnie walks out to the Taurus, then stops and looks up at the sky.

EXT. DARKO HOUSE DRIVEWAY – NEXT

The Time Portal begins to form above the house.

Donnie touches his stomach . . . feeling sick once again.

Donnie then steps into the car, where Gretchen sits in the passenger seat. He turns on the engine and peels out of the driveway.

INT. FORD TAURUS – EARLY MORNING

Donnie drives the Taurus up Carpathian Ridge.

EXT. CARPATHIAN RIDGE – EARLY MORNING (5:30 AM)

Donnie sits on the roof of the Taurus, looking out.

He smiles, lighting a cigarette.

DONNIE
28 days, 6 hours, 42 minutes, 12 seconds. We're almost home.

EXT. SKY – NEXT

We see the Time Portal in the distance forming.

INT. FLIGHT 2806 – DAWN (6 AM)

Samantha Darko is fast asleep. Her head rests on Rose's shoulder.

She looks out of the window at the rising sun.

EXT. DARKO HOUSE – DAWN

The Portal continues to form above the Darko house.

Police cars pull up in front of the house.

EXT. CARPATHIAN RIDGE – DAWN

Donnie continues to stare out at the canyon.

EXT. SKY – NEXT

We see the Time Portal once again.

INT. FORD TAURUS – NEXT

Donnie steps off the hood and gets into the car.

He takes Gretchen's hand.

INT. FLIGHT 2806 – NEXT

On the plane Rose looks out of the window as the jet wing explodes (audio only . . . we don't see it). She screams out as the cabin shakes violently.

EXT. DARKO HOUSE – DAWN

The Time Portal continues to form over the house.

EXT. SKY – NEXT

The left jet engine from Flight 2806 falls downward through the sky. Beneath it the Portal forms itself.

EXT. SKY – NEXT

The falling jet engine approaches the hexagonal plate of light which accelerates downwards . . . forming a tunnel with walls made of swirling liquid marble.

The jet engine passes into the hexagonal plate.

INT./EXT. VARIOUS

In a series of inter-velometer time-lapse shots . . . the entire suburban landscape retreats backward in a fury of speed.

Shot 1: time-lapse of the mongrel statue.

Shot 2: time-lapse of the main school hallway.

Shot 3: time-lapse of the main school building.

Shot 4: time-lapse of neighbourhood street/Darko house.

INT. FOYER – NIGHT

We Steadicam up the stairs.

INT. DONNIE'S ROOM – NIGHT

We move towards Donnie's empty bed.

Title card:

OCTOBER 2 1988

INT. VARIOUS BEDROOMS – NIGHT (1:30 AM)

Dr Thurman wakes up.

Jim Cunningham wakes up . . . sobbing.

Kitty Farmer wakes up . . . coming to a horrible realisation.

Karen Pomeroy and Dr Monnitoff wake up together.

Cherita Chen wakes up.

EXT. SKY – NIGHT (1:30 AM)

The jet engine falls silently through the night down towards the Darko house . . . having travelled back in time.

INT. DONNIE'S ROOM – NEXT

Donnie wakes up. He is laughing hysterically.

The engine crashes through his ceiling . . . engulfing the room.

INT. FAMILY ROOM – NEXT

Eddie jumps up from the La-Z-Boy . . . startled awake by the impact.

INT. MASTER BEDROOM – NEXT

Rose sits up in bed, hearing the crash.

ROSE

Eddie?

INT. FOYER – NEXT

Elizabeth leans against the wall screaming.

INT. DONNIE'S ROOM – NEXT

The mammoth jet engine has plummeted all the way down through the house, creating a cavernous hole that splits Donnie's room in half. The smoke from the wreckage begins to clear.

Above the engine is Donnie . . . impaled through the stomach by a wooden beam that was once part of the floor beneath his bed. There is blood gushing from his mouth, as his face is contorted into the expression that could almost be a smile.

EXT. NEIGHBOURHOOD STREET – MORNING (11 AM)

The same disaster scene as before . . . only more media, more neighbours, and a Coroner. People stand around in shock . . . disbelief.

From the other end of the street, a girl comes riding along on a bike . . . slowly taking in the entire scene. She pulls up to the kerb where a kid named David (eleven) is standing around.

It is Gretchen Ross.

GRETCHEN

Hi . . . what's going on here?

DAVID

Horrible accident. My neighbour . . . he got killed.

GRETCHEN

What happened?

DAVID

He got smooshed. By a jet engine.

She stares at the house, where paramedics wheel a body out of the front door.

GRETCHEN

What was his name?

DAVID

Donnie. Donnie Darko.

They stare at the front yard for a while. We see Elizabeth. We see Eddie, carrying Samantha . . . who is crying.

I feel bad for his family.

GRETCHEN
(*long beat*)

Yeah.

DAVID

Did you know him?

She stares at the family for several moments . . . and then shakes her head slowly as if trying to locate a memory that is slipping away.

GRETCHEN

No.

Rose, leaning against a tree while smoking a cigarette, notices them. She seems to recognise Gretchen . . . from somewhere in the vast reservoir of her memory.

She waves at them.

They wave back.

Fade out.

The End.

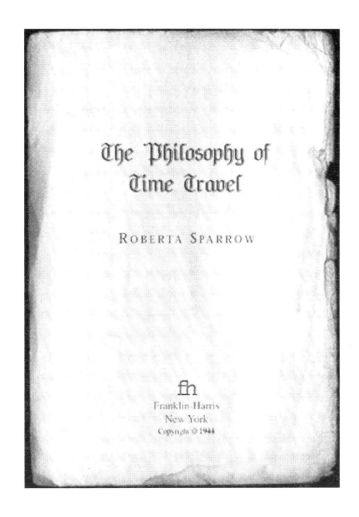

The Philosophy of
Time Travel

ROBERTA SPARROW

fh
Franklin Harris
New York
Copyright © 1944

foreword

J would like to thank the sisters of the Saint John Chapter in Alexandria, Virginia for their support in my decision.

By the grace of God, they are:

Sister Eleanor Lewis
Sister Francesca Godard
Sister Helen Davis
Sister Catherine Arnold
Sister Mary Lee Pond
Sister Virginia Wessex

This intent of this short book is for it to be used as a simple and direct guide in a time of great danger.

I pray that this is merely a work of fiction.

If it is not, then I pray for you, the reader of this book.

If I am still alive when the events foretold in these pages occur, then I hope that you will find me before it is too late.

Roberta Ann Sparrow
October, 1944

Chapter One

The Tangent Universe

The Primary Universe is fraught with great peril.
War, plague, famine and natural disaster are common.
Death comes to us all.

The Fourth Dimension of Time is a stable costruct,
though it is not impenetrable.

Incidents when the fabric of the fourth dimesion
becomes corrupted are incredibly rare.

If a Tangent Universe occurs, it will be highly
unstable, sustaining itself for no longer than several
weeks.

Eventually it will collapse upon itself, forming a
black hole within the Primary Universe capable of
destroying all existence.

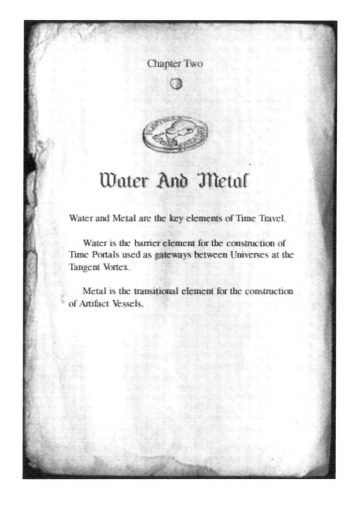

Chapter Two

Water And Metal

Water and Metal are the key elements of Time Travel.

Water is the barrier element for the construction of Time Portals used as gateways between Universes at the Tangent Vortex.

Metal is the transitional element for the construction of Artifact Vessels.

Chapter Four

The Artifact And
The Living

When a Tangent Universe occurs, those living nearest to the Vortex will find themselves at the epicenter of a dangerous new world.

Artifacts provide the first sign that a Tangent Universe has occured.

If an Artifact occurs, the Living will retrieve it with great interest and curiosity. Artifacts are formed from metal, such as an Arrowhead from an ancient Mayan civilization, or a Metal Sword from Medievel Europe.

Artifacts returned to the Primary Universe are often linked to religious Iconography, as their appearance on Earth seems to defy logical explaination.

Divine Intervention is deemed the only logical conclusion for the appearance of the Artifact.

Chapter Six

The Living Receiver

The Living Receiver is chosen to guide the Artifact into postion for its journey back to the Primary Universe.

No one knows how or why a Receiver will be chosen.

The Living Receiver is often blessed with a Fourth Dimensional Powers. These include increased strength, telekenesis, mind control, and the ability to conjure fire and water.

The Living Receiver is often tormented by terrifying dreams, visions and auditory hallucinations during his time within the Tangent Universe.

Those surrounding the Living Receiver, known as the Manipulated, will fear him and try to destroy him.

Chapter Seven

The Manipulated Living

The Manipulated Living are often the close friends and neighbors of the Living Receiver.

They are prone to irrational, bizarre, and often violent behavior. This is the unfortunate result of their task, which is to assist the Living Receiver in returning the Artifact to the Primary Universe.

The Manipulated Living will do anything to save themselves from Oblivion.

Chapter Ten

The Manipulated Dead

The Manipulated Dead are more powerful than the Living Receiver. If a person dies within the Tangent Dimension, they are able to contact the Living Receiver through the Fourth Dimensional Construct.

The Fourth Dimensional Construct is made of Water.

The Manipulated Dead will manipulate the Living Receiver using the Fourth Dimensional Construct (see Appendix A and B).

The Manipulated Dead will often set an Ensurance Trap for the Living Receiver to ensure that the Artifact is returned safely to the Primary Universe.

If the Ensurance Trap is successful, the Living Receiver is left with no choice but to use his Fourth Dimensional Power to send the Artifact back in time into the Primary Universe before the Black Hole collapses upon itself.

Chapter Twelve

Dreams

When the Manipulated awaken from their Journey into the Tangent Universe, they are often haunted by the experience in their dreams.

Many of them will not remember.

Those who do remember the Journey are often overcome with profound remorse for the regretful actions buried within their Dreams, the only physical evidence buried within the Artifact itself; all that remains from the lost world.

Ancient myth tells us of the Mayan Warrior killed by an Arrowhead that had fallen from a cliff, where there was no Army, no enemy to be found.

We are told of the Medievel Knight mysteriously impaled by the sword he had not yet built.

We are told that these things occur for a reason.

Appendix A

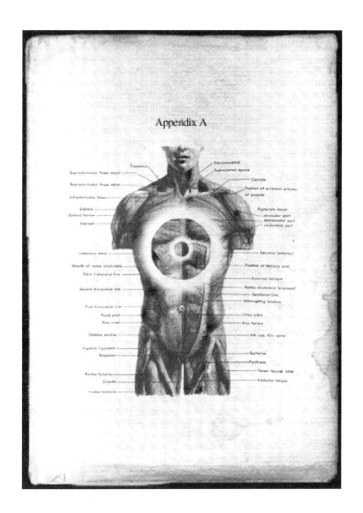

Appendix B

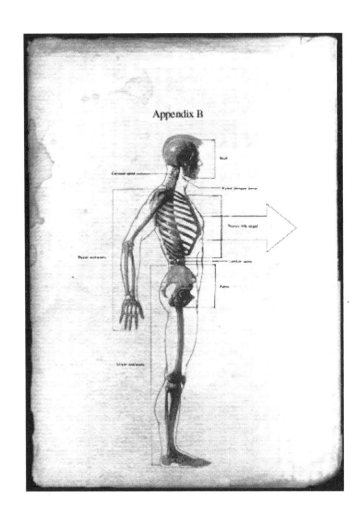

Notes

LIVING RECEIVER
    FRANK DARKO

MANIPULATED DEAD
    FRANK ANDERSON
    GRETCHEN ROSS (NOT HER REAL NAME)

MANIPULATED LIVING
    EDWARD DARKO
    ROSE DARKO
    ELIZABETH DARKO
    SAMANTHA DARKO
    KATHERINE FARMER
    ELIZABETH FARMER
    JIM CUNNINGHAM (DIED OCTOBER 11, 1988)
    KENNETH MONNITOFF
    KAREN POMEROY
    LARRY COLE
    CHERITA CHEN
    SETH DEVLIN
    RICKY DANFORTH
    JOANIE JAMES
    SUSAN BATES
    SUSAN BAILEY
    SEAN SMITH
    LEROY JONES
    MICHAEL CARTER
    LINDA CONNIE
    ROBERTA SPARROW

119

Images from the Film

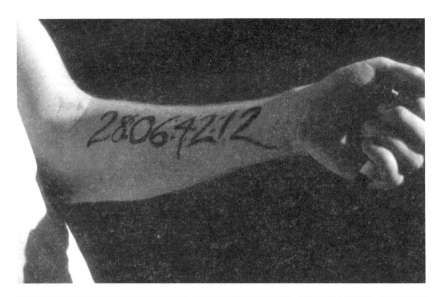

Sketches from the Film

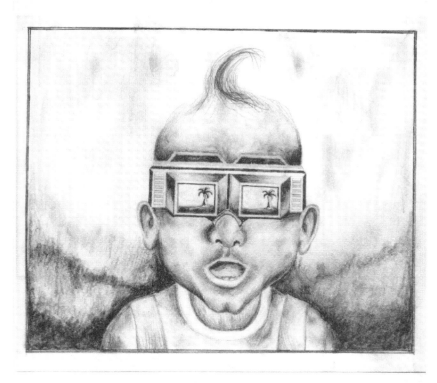

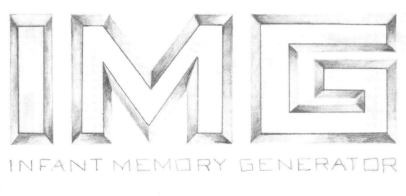

Richard Kelly's original drawing of the Infant Memory Generator.

Above: the Frank drawing
that appears in the film.
Left: one of the original Frank
mask sketches drawn by
Kelly, as featured in the film.

138

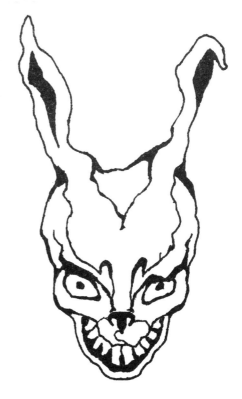

Two more of the Frank mask
sketches that were used to design
the mould for the mask.

139

'I would like to tell you a story about a young man whose life was destroyed by the instruments of fear.'

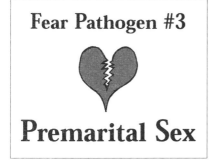

Opposite page, top: the Jim Cunningham auditorium scene, followed by the 'His Name is Frank' slide show that was eventully cut from the scene.

The painting created by Jay Kelly featured in the therapist scenes
with Katharine Ross.

Images from
'They Made Me Do It'
Exhibition

'THEY MADE ME DO IT'

Exhibition featured work by

ASTAK, BLEACH, CHU, COREY, DANE, DREPH, INSA, SHUCKS,
SNUG, SOLO ONE, SONIA, TEMPER, TIZER AND WISHI

These artists, emerging from the UK graffiti scene,
were asked to complete a piece of work on canvas inspired
by the film in 6 hours, 42 minutes and 12 seconds.
The show ran for 28 days in dreambagsjaguarshoes, London.

The exhibition space with the countdown board to the left.

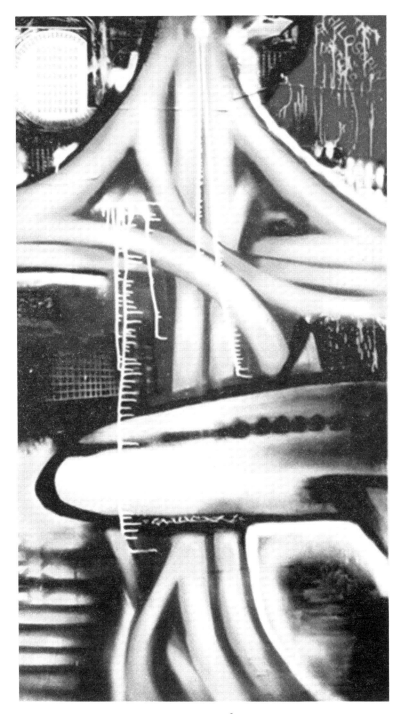

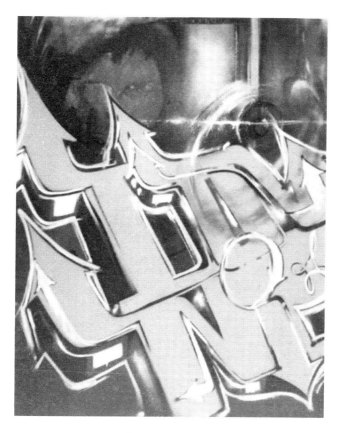

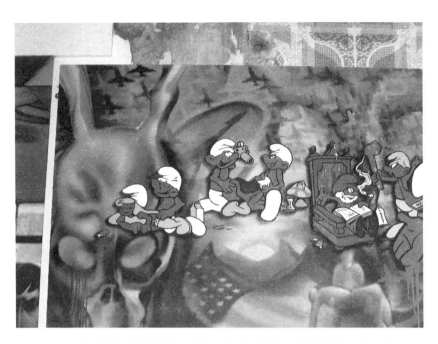

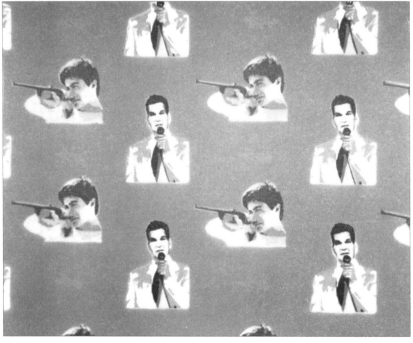